THE HEREFORD PLAYS

General Editor: E. R. Wood

Henrik Ibsen

An Enemy of the People

English adaptation by
MAX FABER

with an Introduction by
MARTIN ESSLIN

HEINEMANN EDUCATIONAL BOOKS
LONDON

Heinemann Educational Books Ltd
22 Bedford Square, London WC1B 3HH

LONDON EDINBURGH MELBOURNE AUCKLAND
HONG KONG SINGAPORE KUALA LUMPUR NEW DELHI
NAIROBI JOHANNESBURG IBADAN
EXETER (NḢ) KINGSTON PORT OF SPAIN

ISBN 0 435 22463 8

Translation © Max Faber 1967
Introduction © Martin Esslin 1967

First published in the *Hereford Plays Series* 1967
Reprinted 1967, 1969, 1972, 1975, 1977, 1981, 1982

Printed in Great Britain by
Spottiswoode Ballantyne Ltd.
Colchester and London

Contents

Introduction

It was from Rome, on 23 November 1881, that Ibsen wrote to his publisher, F. Hegel: 'I am busy with plans for a new comedy in four acts, a work which I had in mind before, but which I laid aside because *Ghosts* forced itself on me and demanded all my attention'. That play, which eventually grew to five acts, was *An Enemy of the People*. On 21 June 1882 Ibsen announced to Hegel that the play was finished: 'Yesterday I completed my new play. It is titled *An Enemy of the People* and is in five acts. I am still uncertain as to whether I should call it a comedy or a straight drama. It has many of the characteristics of comedy but it also has a serious theme . . .' On 9 September 1882 Ibsen sent Hegel the last section of the final manuscript: 'I have enjoyed writing this play,' he wrote from Gossensass, his Tyrolean mountain retreat, 'and I feel quite lost and lonely now that it is out of my hands. Dr Stockmann and I got on so very well together; we agree on so many subjects. But the doctor is more muddle-headed than I am; and moreover he has other peculiarities that permit him to say things which would not be taken so well if I myself said them. . . .'

In fact Ibsen did *not* call *An Enemy of the People* a comedy, but sub-titled it simply 'A Play'. Too much serious matter, too much bitterness had crept into it while he was writing it, under the influence of the storm and scandal that had followed the publication of *Ghosts*. And so Dr Stockmann did indeed become a mouthpiece of his author and the play a very personal declaration – Ibsen's defiant answer to the critics who accused him of being a corrupter of youth, a fanatic who threatened the peace of society by exposing its hidden shames and sources of infection.

An Enemy of the People is Ibsen's most directly *political* play. In most of the other realistic plays of his middle period Ibsen deals with social rather than political problems. But here he boldly tackles the municipal politics of a Norwegian town and exposes the hypocrisy and cowardice of the very circles who had seemed his natural allies, the liberals, the progressives, the democrats. It is they, here represented by the town's newspaper *The Herald* and its editor Hovstad, who 'go on proclaiming day after day the false doctrine that it's the masses, the multitude, the "solid majority" who are the keepers of liberal doctrine and morality! – and that vice, corruption and depravity flow from culture. . . . Fortunately, the idea that culture is demoralizing is just another fabrication that's been handed down to us! No, it's ignorance, poverty and dirt that do the devil's work . . .!' More than eighty years after Ibsen wrote *An Enemy of the People* these are still highly topical sentiments.

In Ibsen's hand the most prosaic subject turned into a structure of powerful symbolic images. The infectious waste products that flow from the tannery into the water of the public baths in Stockmann's home town become a telling metaphor of the lies, the hypocrisies, and the puritanism that Ibsen so hated. 'A community that lives on deceit,' cries Stockmann at the climax of the play, the public meeting in the Fourth Act, ' . . . ought to be razed to the ground. All men who live by lies should be exterminated – like vermin!'

Dr Stockmann utters these radical opinions in the white heat of passion, when he has been intolerably provoked. And Ibsen was right when he said that his hero was somewhat more muddle-headed than he himself. No wonder a good American democrat like Arthur Miller who made a well-known adaptation of *An Enemy of the People* felt compelled to tone down some of the seemingly anti-democratic opinions voiced by Dr Stockmann and to argue that its message lies in a plea for the protection of unpopular minorities. Ibsen certainly makes that last point, but his view is less optimistic, far more bitter and resigned than Miller's. He was fully aware of the tragic position of the man of vision, insight and genius in a society where the majority must, of necessity, be less intelligent, less perceptive and more cowardly than the lonely vanguard who can see farther and deeper than the masses and is capable of facing unpleasant facts more boldly. 'You are, of course, right,' he wrote to Georg Brandes in June 1883, 'when you say that we must all work for the spread of our ideas. But I maintain that a fighter in the intellectual vanguard cannot possibly gather a majority around him. In ten years the majority will possibly occupy the standpoint which Dr Stockmann held at the public meeting. But during those ten years the doctor will not have been standing still; he will still be at least ten years ahead of the majority. The majority, the mass, the mob will never catch up with him; and he can never have the majority with him. As regards myself at least, I am quite aware of such unceasing progress. At the point where I stood when I wrote each of my books there now stands a tolerably compact crowd; but I myself am no longer there. I am elsewhere; farther ahead, I hope.'

So it is not only that Dr Stockmann happens to be unpopular as the herald of one particular, and peculiarly unpleasant truth in one particular case. The holder of the truth, the man who can see the essence of the situation, is *bound* to be unpopular, and bound to remain so, even if the masses catch up with his ideas in due course. That is the meaning of Stockmann's final summing up, the oft-quoted line: 'The strongest man in the world is he who stands alone!'

There is a certain arrogance, a certain aristocratic intolerance in this attitude. *An Enemy of the People* is not a difficult play, it is built on the model of the most successful kind of nineteenth-century French drama; but its subject matter is closely akin to Ibsen's most ambitious and most difficult work, the great poem *Brand*, the hero of which also is a man who feels strongest because he stands alone and whose stubborn determination not to yield an inch brings ruin to all around him. In a certain sense Dr Stockmann is a popularized version of Brand, reduced in size and without Brand's fanatical destructiveness. At the end of *An Enemy of the People* we are left without any indication whether Dr Stockmann's courageous stand, his decision to face his adversaries on his own home ground rather than to move elsewhere and start afresh, will in fact bring ruin to his family. There are grounds to assume that Ibsen wanted the audience to be reassured on this point. Writing to Edvard Fallesen, the director of the Royal Theatre at Copenhagen who was about to stage the play, Ibsen expressly asked that Captain Horster, one of the few who remain staunch supporters of Dr Stockmann, should be played as a *young* man, so that in the fifth act it should be possible to infer that an 'intimate and warm friendship' might be about to grow up between him and Stockmann's daughter Petra, thus compensating her for the painful disappointment she suffered in the editor, Hovstad, in whose progressive ideas she had previously shown a more than merely theoretical interest. That is why *An Enemy of the People*, though not a comedy any more, still keeps clear of being a tragedy. Dr Stockmann, unlike Brand, will survive; he will, indeed, eventually win his point, even though, by that time, he will again be ahead of the masses and therefore have incurred unpopularity for some other reason.

It is highly characteristic of Ibsen that he could also see the other point of view. His very next play, *The Wild Duck*, demonstrates the destructiveness, the humourlessness of a fanatic of the truth, Gregers Werle, who in destroying the lie by which the Ekdals live also destroys their happiness. This is the other side of Brand and to some extent also of Dr Stockmann. But there is also an essential difference between Gregers Werle and Dr Stockmann: while the former's concern is with the destruction of a *private* lie which does not harm society, the latter causes trouble and unhappiness by insisting on exposing a social evil based on the *collective* lie of a whole community.

Many of Ibsen's attacks on the social evils of his time have inevitably dated – for the social conditions he criticized, notably the status of women and the squeamishness of the nineteenth century about the open discussion of sexual and moral problems, have undergone a radical change for the better since Ibsen's day. Being a political rather than a social play *An Enemy of the People* has curiously, at first glance almost paradoxically, escaped this process of dating. On closer reflection this will appear natural enough. While social conditions change from century to century, politics remains essentially the same. The struggle for power, for the support of the majority in one form or another, these were the essence of politics then as they are now and as they have been in any other historical epoch. Always politicians have been involved in the dilemma that to retain their power and influence they must serve the sectional interests of their supporters, even if they can clearly discern the long-term advantage of short-term sacrifices on their part. Today as in Ibsen's time the politician who tries to win his election by concentrating on the cost of living in his own constituency while neglecting some major world problems of mass starvation or war in other continents, re-enacts the dilemma of Dr Stockmann's brother the mayor, and of Hovstad, the editor. And Mr Aslaksen, the leader of the ratepayers association, is the eternal symbol of the electorate themselves for whom all long-term social, cultural and ideological issues ultimately reduce themselves to pounds, shillings and pence. The clarity of the vision, the economy of the technique with which Ibsen has succeeded in compressing these eternal elements of all politics into the compass of a small, compact community, of a single dramatic conflict, is a truly astonishing proof of his genius.

This is also clearly the reason why this particular play of Ibsen's has so frequently been revived, so frequently been adapted to fit into different national idioms and milieux. Whether in American, German, English North Country (as in a recent radio adaptation by Henry Livings) or Norwegian, *An Enemy of the People* will always prove itself as one of the archetypal images of political conflict, even if it is not Ibsen's most poetic, or his most profound play.

It is also a play which presents the producer with a healthy challenge in one of Ibsen's relatively rare crowd scenes, the public meeting in the fourth act. Ibsen was very anxious that the numerous small parts in that scene should be cast with highly accomplished actors, so that the crowd itself, the stage image of the mob Dr Stockmann – and Ibsen – confront, should be seen to be composed of individuals, not generalized types.

Apart from this one scene, *An Enemy of the People* has the simplicity of all technically perfect structures. That the two main antagonists, the medical officer of health and the mayor, should be brothers is a fine poetic stroke: it deepens the purely political conflict into a battle within one family, with an echo of the struggle of Cain and Abel.

The two journalists from *The Herald*, Hovstad and Billing, both young men, both progressives, play a particularly vital part in the mechanics of the play. For while the mayor is clearly shown as a reactionary, and Mr Aslaksen as a 'moderate', i.e. a cautious and somewhat cowardly supporter of liberal ideas from the start, these two young men are Dr Stockmann's intimates and admirers; their defection comes as a surprise, the mercenary nature of their attitude (also shown in the episode of the English novel Petra has been asked to translate) is a painful revelation. As always in Ibsen's plays the characters balance each other in such a way that the features of each act as a foil to those of his opposite number. Each character has his definite function in the plot. It is the elegance of the structure that it rests on the utmost economy of means. The Ibsen of *Peer Gynt* may have been an exuberant romantic. The Ibsen of *An Enemy of the People* is a master of the 'well-made play'.

MARTIN ESSLIN

CHARACTERS

DR THOMAS STOCKMANN, *Town Medical Officer of Health*

MRS KATHERINE STOCKMANN, *his wife*

PETRA, *their daughter, a schoolmistress*

EILIF
MORTEN } *their sons – aged thirteen and ten respectively*

PETER STOCKMANN, *Dr Stockmann's elder brother – Mayor, Chief Constable, and Chairman of the Municipal Baths Committee, etc.*

MORTEN KIIL, *a master-tanner*

MR HOVSTAD, *editor of* The Herald

MR BILLING, *the sub-editor*

CAPTAIN HORSTER, *a ship's master*

MR ASLAKSEN, *a master-printer*

A group of MEN and WOMEN of mixed social standing, and a number of SCHOOLBOYS.

The action of the play passes during four consecutive days in early spring of the year 1882, at a coastal town in Southern Norway.

SYNOPSIS OF SCENES

ACT ONE

Dr Thomas Stockmann's sitting-room – evening. A modestly appointed, neatly furnished and simply decorated room. Up-right, a door leads to the hall – another down-right, to Dr Stockmann's consulting-room, and a third up-left, opposite the hall door, leads to the rest of the house. Down-left-centre, a stove – and down-left, a sofa with a mirror on the wall above it, and in front of it an oval table with a cloth on it. In the rear wall, open communicating-doors lead to the dining-room, which is also plainly furnished with, centre, a dining-table with a lamp upon it, and chairs.

MR BILLING is sitting at the dining-table, with a napkin tucked under his chin, and MRS KATHERINE STOCKMANN is standing by the table and placing a large plate of roast beef in front of him. The other chairs round the table are pushed back and the table itself untidy and disarrayed, as after a meal.

KATHERINE: Well, if you will arrive an hour late for supper, Mr Billing – you mustn't mind it if the meat's a bit cold . . .

MR BILLING (*eating*): Oh, that's all right – it's very nice indeed – it's delicious. . . .

KATHERINE: You know how my husband always likes to have his meals at the right time . . .

MR BILLING: Oh, don't worry about me, Mrs Stockmann. As a matter of fact, I quite like eating alone – I enjoy my food better when I can have it in peace and quiet . . .

KATHERINE: Oh well, so long as you enjoy it, that's the chief thing— (*Breaks off and listens in the direction of the hall door.*) I shouldn't be a bit surprised if that's Mr Hovstad . . .

MR BILLING (*with his mouth full*): No – nor should I . . .

Enter MR PETER STOCKMANN by hall door, wearing an overcoat, a peaked cap with gold-braid, and carrying a stick.

PETER: Good evening, Katherine, my dear. . . .

KATHERINE (*crossing to sitting-room*): Oh, it's you, is it? . . . Good evening, Peter – do come in. How nice of you to come and see us like this . . .

PETER: Oh, I happened to be passing, so I thought I'ld— (*Looks towards dining-room.*) Oh, but I see you've got company . . .

KATHERINE (*slightly embarrassedly*): Oh no, not really – er – that is, not what you'd call company – just someone that's looked in . . . (*Hurriedly.*) But what about you? – Won't you come and sit down and have something to eat, too, now that you're here?

PETER: I? – No, no, thank you, I don't think I will . . . Besides – good gracious! – roast beef at this hour! – With my digestion! – Why, I shouldn't sleep a wink!

KATHERINE: Oh, but surely just once in a way . . .

PETER: No, no – thanks all the same, my dear – but not for me . . . I believe in a nice cup of tea and a few slices of bread and butter of an evening – which is not only much better for you, y'know, but costs considerably less . . .

KATHERINE (*smiling*): Oh, you mustn't think Thomas and I are extravagant just because . . .

PETER: Oh, I don't think *you* are, Katherine – not for a moment . . . (*Gestures towards study.*) Isn't he in then?

KATHERINE: No – he's just taken the boys out for a little walk after supper . . .

PETER: I shouldn't have thought that was a very wise thing to do on a full stomach! (*Listens.*) Ah – I expect that's him . . .

KATHERINE: No, he wouldn't be back yet . . . (*Knock on hall door.*) Come in!

Enter MR HOVSTAD *from hall.*

KATHERINE: Oh, it's you, Mr Hovstad!

MR HOVSTAD: Yes – I'm sorry to be so late, but I got held up at the printer's . . . Oh, good evening, Mr Mayor . . .

PETER (*bowing somewhat stiffly*): Good evening, Mr Hovstad. You're here on business, I take it?

MR HOVSTAD: Yes, partly. About an article for the paper . . .

PETER: I thought as much. They tell me my brother's been writing quite a few articles for *The Herald* lately . . .

MR HOVSTAD: Yes – he generally likes to make use of *The Herald* when he feels particularly strongly about anything; and, of course, we're only too pleased . . .

KATHERINE (*to Mr Hovstad*): But won't you—? (*Gestures towards dining-room.*)

PETER: Oh, not that I blame him for airing his views in any quarter where he's likely to be appreciated . . . And, personally, I've nothing against your paper, y'know, Mr Hovstad. . . .

MR HOVSTAD: No, I should hope not, indeed!

PETER: I think one may safely say that there's as fine a spirit of tolerance, mutual understanding and fair-mindedness here in this town as you'll find anywhere – in fact, public spirit has never been so high as it is today! – Thanks to this great new common interest of ours – an interest in which every right-minded citizen is equally concerned . . .

MR HOVSTAD: Oh yes – the Spa Baths . . .

PETER: Exactly! – Our magnificent new municipal baths! Mark my words, Mr Hovstad – the whole future of this town – as a really popular seaside resort – centres round those baths! There's no doubt about it!

KATHERINE: Yes – that's exactly what Thomas says . . .

PETER: Why, just look at the development that's taken place already – even in the last two years! There's been more money in the town – business has improved – the value of property rises every day. As a result there's more life altogether!

MR HOVSTAD: Yes – and there's nothing like the unemployment there was, either. Don't forget that!

PETER: Yes, and that's another thing! We've seen quite a

little reduction in the Poor Rate – much to the relief of those who have to pay it! – And it will go down still more, if only we get a good summer this year, with a steady stream of visitors and a good influx of invalids to establish the reputation of the baths!

MR HOVSTAD: And, from all I hear, I should say there's every prospect of it!

PETER: Well, things certainly look most promising. We're getting more inquiries for accommodation every day – some of the boarding-houses are booking already . . .

MR HOVSTAD: Then the Doctor's article'll appear just at the right moment . . .

PETER: Why? Has he written another, then?

MR HOVSTAD: No – this is one he wrote during the winter – mostly about the health-giving properties of the baths, and the excellent sanitary conditions of the town and so on. But I thought it better to hold it over . . .

PETER: Ah – I suppose he put his foot in it somewhere. Was that it?

MR HOVSTAD: Not at all. – I simply decided to keep it till the spring, when people are beginning to think about their summer holidays . . .

PETER: Quite right, Mr Hovstad – very sensible.

KATHERINE: Yes, I don't think there's anything Thomas wouldn't do when it comes to the baths!

PETER: Well, after all, it's expected of him, y'know, Katherine – as the Town Medical Officer of Health . . . !

MR HOVSTAD: Yes, and not only that – but he practically created them.

PETER: Did he? – Really? – Certainly, I've heard that opinion expressed in certain quarters, Mr Hovstad. All the same, I should like to believe that I, too, played a modest part in the undertaking . . .

KATHERINE: Thomas always says so – I know.

MR HOVSTAD: But who denies it, Mr Mayor? Everybody

knows that you were responsible for putting the plan into operation and for organizing it on a practical basis . . . All I meant was that the idea came from the Doctor originally . . . !

PETER: Oh, the idea – yes! I don't dispute that for a moment! My brother's always been a man of ideas – unfortunately! Y'know, it's one thing to have ideas, Mr Hovstad, but quite another to put them into practice! – When it comes to that we want a man of action! And I should have thought that in this house at least—

KATHERINE: But Peter, dear—

MR HOVSTAD: Now how can you—?

KATHERINE: Won't you go in and have something to eat, Mr Hovstad? – I'm sure my husband won't be long . . .

MR HOVSTAD: Well, thank you, Mrs Stockmann – perhaps I will then – just a bite. . . . (*Crosses into dining-room.*)

PETER (*sotto voce*): Curious thing – they're all the same, these country bumpkins – no tact!

KATHERINE: Oh, I shouldn't worry about it. Surely you and Thomas can share the credit between you as brothers?

PETER: Well, I should have thought so; but it seems that some people aren't satisfied with just a share!

KATHERINE: Oh, stuff and nonsense! – You and Thomas get on fine together, you know you do! (*Listens.*) Ah – there he is now, I think. (*Crosses and opens hall door.*)

DR STOCKMANN (*off-stage – laughing and talking*): Ah – hullo, Kate – look, I've got another visitor for you! Isn't that grand? Come in, Captain Horster – hang your coat up on that peg over there! Oh, of course, I forgot you don't wear one! – well, hang your hat up then! Would you believe it, Kate – I met him down the street and I almost had to threaten him with violence before I could get him to come in! (*Enter* CAPT HORSTER, *and bows to Katherine.*) In you go, boys. D'you know they're both starving again! – they've got appetites like young horses! . . . You'll sit down and have a slice of roast beef, won't you, Captain Horster? Come along now – it's good for you! (*Shepherds Capt Horster almost forcibly into the dining-room. EILIF and MORTEN follow.*)

KATHERINE: But Thomas, look who's—

DR STOCKMANN (*turning*): Why, it's you, Peter! (*Crosses and shakes him by the hand.*) Well, this is a pleasant surprise!

PETER: I can't stay long, I'm afraid – I only dropped in for a few moments . . .

DR STOCKMANN: Rubbish! We're going to have some toddy in a minute! – You haven't forgotten about it, have you, Kate?

KATHERINE: No, of course not – I've got the water on; it should be boiling by now . . . I'll go and see . . . (*Crosses to dining-room.*)

PETER: Toddy, too—!

DR STOCKMANN: Yes. Now let's sit down and make ourselves comfortable, shall we?

PETER: Thanks – but you know I don't hold with drinking parties . . . !

DR STOCKMANN: Oh, don't be silly, this isn't going to be a drinking party. We're just having a glass of toddy, that's all!

PETER: Well, that's as may be. (*Gesturing towards dining-room.*) It's extraordinary the way they manage to stuff like that! – I don't know where they put it all!

DR STOCKMANN (*rubbing his hands*): Ah, but doesn't it do your heart good to see young people eat, eh? Y'know, they're always hungry those two! – and that's as it should be! Plenty of good red meat, that's what they need – to give 'em strength, build 'em up! After all, they're the ones that are going to revolutionize the future, Peter!

PETER: I shouldn't have thought it wanted revolutionizing!

DR STOCKMANN: Ah – you wait and see what they think about it, when the time comes! Not that we shall live to see it, of course. – A couple of old fogies like us . . .

PETER: Really, Thomas – I should hardly describe myself as an old fogey . . .

DR STOCKMANN: Oh, you mustn't take any notice of me, Peter. It's only my fun! I like to feel new life around me. We're living in a wonderful time! – It's almost like standing on the threshold of a new era. . . .

PETER: You think so, do you?

DR STOCKMANN: Well, naturally, it wouldn't be so apparent to you as it is to me. You've lived here all your life. You're used to it. But I've been buried up north at the back of beyond for years, where I hardly ever saw a strange face, let alone met anyone I could talk to! – And settling here like this has had much the same effect on me as suddenly finding myself right in the middle of a capital city . . .

PETER: Well, but a capital city—

DR STOCKMANN: Oh, I know there's no comparison, of course – everything here's on a very much smaller scale, compared with even the big towns. But there's life here – promise – plenty to work and strive for, and that's the great thing . . . (*Calls.*) Kate – are there any letters for me?

KATHERINE (*from dining-room*): No, dear – the postman hasn't been yet . . .

DR STOCKMANN: And then, to be getting more money, Peter! – That's something one really appreciates, when one's had to exist – as we've had to – on a mere pittance . . .

PETER: Oh, I can hardly—

DR STOCKMANN: Yes, you've no idea how tight things were sometimes. And now we're living in the lap of luxury! Today, for instance, we had roast beef for dinner – and, not only that, we've had it for supper as well! Come on – won't you try a little bit? – Or, at least, come and see if you like the look of it . . .

PETER: No – no, thank you!

DR STOCKMANN: Oh, well . . . D'you see we've got a new tablecloth . . . !

PETER: Yes – I noticed it.

DR STOCKMANN: Did you notice the new lamp-shade, too?

– Kate saved up for both of them. They make a wonderful difference to the room – don't you think? Look – just stand over there for a moment . . . No – not there – further over . . . There! – See how the light falls? . . . Don't you think that's quite artistic . . .?

PETER: Yes, it's very nice – if you can afford luxuries like that . . .

DR STOCKMANN: Oh, but I can now. Kate says I earn almost as much as she spends!

PETER: Almost – I'm not surprised!

DR STOCKMANN: Ah, but a medical man must live in some sort of style! Why a mere County Court judge spends more per annum than I do!

PETER: I dare say. After all, an important member of the judiciary . . .

DR STOCKMANN: Well, an ordinary merchant, then! A man like that spends quite three or four times as much as—

PETER: That's only to be expected. After all, he leads a very different sort of life. . . .

DR STOCKMANN: But I don't waste money, y'know, Peter. Oh, I know I like to do a little bit of entertaining – but I like having my friends around me. I thrive on it. I've lived so long away from it all that I need lively, honest, ambitious young men about the place – and that's what they are, Peter, every one of them, that's sitting in there now and eating his supper! . . . I only wish you got on better with Hovstad—

PETER: That reminds me – Mr Hovstad was telling me he's going to print another article of yours . . .

DR STOCKMANN: Article of mine?

PETER: Yes – about the Spa Baths. One you wrote during the winter.

DR STOCKMANN: Oh, that! Yes, I remember. Oh, I can't let him put that in now.

PETER: Why not? – I should have thought that this was the ideal moment for it.

DR STOCKMANN: Yes, I suppose so – if things were normal . . . (*Crosses room.*)

PETER (*following him with his eyes*): Why? Aren't things normal, then?

DR STOCKMANN (*standing still*): I'm sorry, Peter, but I can't tell you just at the moment – at least not this evening. You see, I don't know myself yet that I'm not mistaken – things may be perfectly normal. Perhaps they are . . . in which case it's merely my imagination . . .

PETER: Well, I must say, you're being very mysterious. Is there anything the matter then? – anything I'm not supposed to know about? Because I should have thought that, as chairman of the baths committee—

DR STOCKMANN: And I should have thought that as – Oh, now don't let's fly off the handle at one another, Peter. . . .

PETER: No, indeed! *I'm* not in the habit of flying off the handle, as you call it! But I've got every right to insist that any plans you have in mind shall be dealt with in a business-like way by the proper authorities! I won't stand for any beating-about-the-bush, or underhand methods!

DR STOCKMANN: Have you ever known me at any time to beat-about-the-bush, or employ underhand methods, Peter?

PETER: No; but you like to go your own sweet way, and that, in a well-ordered community, amounts to much the same thing. You've heard me say this before: it's the duty of the individual to subordinate himself to society, or to be more precise, to the municipal authorities in charge of our civic welfare!

DR STOCKMANN: I dare say. But what the devil has that got to do with me?

PETER: That, my dear Thomas, is just what you don't seem to realize! But one of these days it may cost you dear! So don't say I didn't tell you! Good-bye!

DR STOCKMANN: What *are* you talking about? – You're on the wrong tack altogether, y'know . . .

PETER: I doubt it – I'm usually right. And, in any case, I've no time for—(*Bows towards dining-room.*) Good night, Katherine . . . Good night, gentlemen. . . . (*Exit by hall door.*)

KATHERINE (*crossing from dining-room*): Has he gone, Thomas?

DR STOCKMANN: Yes, and in a lovely temper, too.

KATHERINE: Why? – What have you been saying to him, now, dear?

DR STOCKMANN: Nothing – nothing at all. And, anyhow, he can't expect me to report to him every five minutes about things I'm not even certain of myself!

KATHERINE: What are you supposed to report to him, then?

DR STOCKMANN: H'm – never you mind, Kate . . . I wonder what's happened to that postman – he's usually here by now . . .!

MESSRS HOVSTAD *and* BILLING *and* CAPT HORSTER *have got up from the dining-table and come into the sitting-room.* EILIF *and* MORTEN *follow them.*

MR BILLING (*stretching himself*): Well – one feels a new man after a meal like that! And that's a fact!

MR HOVSTAD: His worship didn't strike me as being in a particularly good mood this evening . . .!

DR STOCKMANN: It's his stomach, y'know – he's one of the worst cases of indigestion I've ever met!

MR HOVSTAD: I should think it was finding the staff of *The Herald* in occupation that really gave him something to digest!

KATHERINE: Oh, but I thought you were getting on quite well with him.

MR HOVSTAD: Yes – but it's only a sort of armistice!

MR BILLING: Exactly! – Armistice is the word!

DR STOCKMANN: Ah, but we must remember that Peter's a lonely old bachelor, poor fellow. He has no home life – only business, more business, and that revolting weak tea he drinks by the gallon! – Now lads, pull up your chairs! – Is that toddy ready, Kate?

KATHERINE (*crossing to dining-room*): Yes – I'm just getting it . . .

DR STOCKMANN: Good! – Now you come and sit over here next to me, Captain Horster – you're the distinguished visitor! Come along now, my lads – make yourselves comfortable! . . .

All sit round table, as KATHERINE *enters with spirit-lamp, decanters, bottles, glasses, etc. on a tray, which she puts down on table.*

KATHERINE: There we are! This is arrack, this is rum, and this is the brandy. So now you can help yourselves . . .!

DR STOCKMANN (*taking a glass*): We will, Kate. – Leave it to us, eh, lads? (*Mixes toddy.*) Now how about a cigar? Eilif, I think you know where the box is – go and get it, there's a good boy! And Morten, you can fetch my pipe. . . . (*Exeunt* EILIF *and* MORTEN *by door right.*) Y'know, I've a shrewd suspicion that young Eilif helps himself to a cigar occasionally, but I pretend not to notice. (*Calls.*) And bring my smoking-cap, Morten. – Kate, go and tell him where it is. . . . (*Enter* EILIF *and* MORTEN *with articles by door right.*) Ah – he's got it – good boy! . . . That's right, hand them round, Eilif! . . . You fellows don't mind if I stick to my pipe – do you? I'm particularly fond of this one – it's a very old friend – it's seen me through many a storm up north! (*They clink glasses.*) Well, jolly good health, everybody! Ah – it's wonderful to be sitting here, I can tell you – warm and cosy like this!

KATHERINE (*sitting and knitting*): When are you sailing again, Captain Horster?

CAPT HORSTER: Oh, sometime next week, I hope.

KATHERINE: Where to? – America this time?

CAPT HORSTER: Yes, I think so.

MR BILLING: Oh, then you won't be here for the municipal elections?

CAPT HORSTER: Why, is there going to be an election, then?

MR BILLING: Yes – you don't mean to say you didn't know?

CAPT HORSTER: No, I don't bother my head about things like that.

MR BILLING: But, surely, you take some interest in public affairs?

CAPT HORSTER: No – they're quite out of my depth.

MR BILLING: Even so, y'know, you ought to vote . . . Every vote counts . . .

CAPT HORSTER: What – even if I don't know what I'm voting for?

MR BILLING: Know? – But there's nothing to know! It's perfectly straightforward! You see, the town's like a ship – everyone must help to steer . . .

CAPT HORSTER: Oh, that may be all right ashore, but it'ld never do at sea!

MR HOVSTAD: Y'know, it's really quite extraordinary how little sailors care about what happens on land!

MR BILLING: Yes – it's incredible!

DR STOCKMANN: Sailors are birds of passage – they're at home in every port. So it's up to us to make up for them, Hovstad. Will there be anything of local interest in to-morrow's *Herald*?

MR HOVSTAD: No, nothing tomorrow. But I'm planning to use your article the day after—

DR STOCKMANN: Oh, hang the article! – You'll have to hold that over for a bit, anyhow, I'm afraid. . . .

MR HOVSTAD: Really? – But we've just the right amount of space; and I should have thought that this was the ideal moment—

DR STOCKMANN: Yes, you may be right about that – but I must still ask you to hold it over. I'll tell you why later . . .

Enter PETRA STOCKMANN *by hall door, wearing a hat and cloak and carrying a bundle of exercise books under her arm.*

PETRA: Oh, good evening. – Good evening.

DR STOCKMANN: Ah, it's you, Petra – good evening, my dear . . .

Greetings are exchanged, and PETRA *puts her hat, cloak and exercise books on a chair by the door.*

PETRA: And to think that you've all been sitting enjoying yourselves, while I've been working my fingers to the bone!

DR STOCKMANN: Well, you come and enjoy yourself, too.

MR BILLING (*to Petra*): May I mix you a glass of toddy?

PETRA (*crossing to table*): No thanks – I'd rather do it myself – you always make it so strong . . . Oh, by the way, Father, I've got a letter for you . . . (*Crosses to where her things are on the chair.*)

DR STOCKMANN: A letter? – From whom?

PETRA (*searching in cloak pocket*): I've no idea. The postman gave it to me as I was going down the road this morning . . .

DR STOCKMANN (*rising and crossing to her*): And you keep me waiting all this time for it!

PETRA: Well, I was late – I simply hadn't the time to run all the way back again. Anyhow, here it is.

DR STOCKMANN (*seizing it*): Good. Let's have a look. (*Examines envelope.*) Yes, this is it! – This is it, all right!

KATHERINE: Is it the one you've been so anxious about, Thomas?

DR STOCKMANN: Yes, it is. I'll just go into the consulting-room and— (*Crosses and pushes open door.*) Have you got a light, Kate? – There's no lamp in here again! . . .

KATHERINE: Yes, there is, dear – on the writing-table, it's turned down low, that's all. . . .

DR STOCKMANN: Oh yes – good . . . good! Excuse me a moment— (*Exit by door right.*)

PETRA: What on earth is it about, Mother?

KATHERINE: Don't ask me. All I know is that for the last two days he's been continually asking about the postman . . .

MR BILLING: A country patient, perhaps . . .

PETRA: Poor Father! – He'll be overworking himself if he's not careful! (*Mixes toddy*.) There – now that should taste all right . . .!

MR HOVSTAD: Have you been teaching at the night-school again this evening?

PETRA (*sipping her drink*): Yes – for a couple of hours . . .

MR BILLING: And four hours this morning at the day-school—

PETRA: Five!

KATHERINE: I see you've brought some exercise books home, dear. – Have you got a lot of correcting to do again tonight, then?

PETRA: Yes, a whole stack of it.

CAPT HORSTER: Then it looks to me as if you'll be over-working yourself too, if you're not careful!

PETRA: Oh, but I like it. You see, you always feel so lovely and tired afterwards.

MR BILLING: And is that a good thing?

PETRA: Oh yes – because then you sleep so much better, and I love my sleep!

MORTEN: Then you must be really awfully wicked, Petra . . .

PETRA: Wicked? – Why?

MORTEN: Yes, doing all that work! Because Mr Rorlund says work's a punishment for our sins!

EILIF (*scornfully*): Oh – what rot! – You're a fathead, if you believe that stuff!

KATHERINE: Now then, Eilif—!

MR BILLING (*laughing*): That's the best thing I've heard for a long time!

MR HOVSTAD: It sounds to me as if we're not very fond of work – eh, Morten?

MORTEN: No, I'm not – I hate it!

MR HOVSTAD: What are you going to be when you grow up?

MORTEN: Oh, I'm going to be a viking!

EILIF: Then you'll have to be a heathen!

MORTEN: Well then, I'll be a heathen!

MR BILLING: That's the idea, Morten I agree with you! I'm on your side! – That's exactly what I say!

KATHERINE (*making signs at him*): Now you know you're not serious, Mr Billing . . .!

MR BILLING: Oh yes, I am – deadly serious! I'm a heathen, and that's a fact! You wait – we shall all be heathens before long!

MORTEN: And then shall we be able to do what we like?

MR BILLING: Well, you see, Morten, it's—

KATHERINE: Now run along, boys – you know you've got your homework to do, before you go to bed!

EILIF: Oh but, Mummy, let me stay up a little longer! – I'm older than Morten!

KATHERINE: No, not you, either. – Off you go now, both of you!

    EILIF *and* MORTEN *say good night to everyone and exeunt left.*

MR HOVSTAD: D'you really think it does the boys any harm to hear things like that, then, Mrs Stockmann?

KATHERINE: Well, I don't know. – Anyhow, I don't like it.

PETRA: Y'know, Mother – I think you're quite wrong.

KATHERINE: Maybe I am – but I still don't like it – and certainly not at home here . . .

PETRA: But, don't you see, Mother, how hypocritical it all is – both at home and at school? . . . At home you mustn't tell children the truth, and at school you have to tell them lies!

CAPT HORSTER: But must you tell them lies?

PETRA: Yes, of course. – Don't you suppose we have to tell them any number of things we don't believe in ourselves?

MR BILLING: Yes, that's perfectly true.

PETRA: If only I had the means I'd start a school of my own – and it would be run on very different lines, I can assure you . . .

CAPT HORSTER: Well, if you're really serious about it, Miss Stockmann, I can provide you with accommodation. Indeed, I should be only too delighted. You know that great barn of a house my father left me – it's practically empty and standing there doing nothing. There's an enormous dining-room on the ground floor that'ld make an excellent school-room . . .

PETRA (*laughing*): Thank you very much, Captain Horster, it's very nice of you – but I don't suppose it's ever likely to happen, unfortunately . . .

MR HOVSTAD: No; I rather fancy Miss Petra is more likely to turn to journalism. By the way, have you had time to look at that serial you promised to translate for us?

PETRA: No, not yet – but I haven't forgotten it, you shall have it soon . . .

Enter DR STOCKMANN *from consulting-room, with an open letter in his hand.*

DR STOCKMANN (*brandishing letter*): I've got some news here that'll shake the town, I can tell you!

MR BILLING: News?

KATHERINE: What, dear?

DR STOCKMANN: A vital discovery, Kate!

MR HOVSTAD: Really?

KATHERINE: Of yours?

DR STOCKMANN: Yes, of mine! (*Paces.*) Now let them call me a crank – if they dare! – *If* they dare! Ha-ha! But they won't, y'know – not this time! – Oh no! . . .

PETRA: But Father, what is it?

DR STOCKMANN: Well, don't rush me, then – and I'll tell you all about it! Oh, if only brother Peter were here now! It just shows how even the best of us can go about jumping to conclusions and making statements, when all the time we're in the dark—

MR HOVSTAD: Why? What d'you mean, Doctor?

DR STOCKMANN (*stopping at table*): Isn't it now an accepted fact that our town is one of the healthiest places in the country?

MR HOVSTAD: Well, of course ...

DR STOCKMANN: One of the finest and most recuperative seaside watering-places along this, or any other, coast? – A place to be thoroughly recommended both to invalids and holiday-makers alike?

KATHERINE: But Thomas dear—

DR STOCKMANN: And haven't we all been praising it up to the skies? Look at the articles I've written about it in *The Herald* – the pamphlets, the brochures, I've—

MR HOVSTAD: Yes, of course, Doctor, but what—?

DR STOCKMANN: The baths, which we've called 'the mainstay of the community' – 'the nerve-centre of the town', and heaven knows what else—

MR BILLING: 'The very heart of our fair city', I remember calling them once in an after-dinner speech—!

DR STOCKMANN: Yes, I'm sure you did. Well – d'you know what they actually are, these marvellous, palatial, highly-praised baths, that have cost so many thousands – d'you know what they are—?

MR HOVSTAD: No—?

KATHERINE: Yes, what, Thomas?

DR STOCKMANN: They're simply a plague-spot!

PETRA: The baths, Father?

KATHERINE (*simultaneously*): Our baths!

MR HOVSTAD (*similarly*): But, Doctor—!

MR BILLING (*similarly*): But – but it's unbelievable!

DR STOCKMANN: I tell you the whole place is a centre of infection! – it's practically a glorified cesspool! and a very serious menace to public health! All that effluent and muck from the tannery up at Molledal – all that stinking stuff! – is actually getting into the pipes and contaminating the water they use in the Pump Room! *And* – what's more – the same poisonous filth finally oozes out on the shore by the break-water . . .

CAPT HORSTER: What – where the bathing-station is?

DR STOCKMANN: Yes, right by the bathing-station!

MR HOVSTAD: But how can you be so certain of all this, Doctor?

DR STOCKMANN: Well, I started by investigating the matter myself – as carefully as I possibly could. Oh, I'd had my suspicions about it for some time. Last season, if you remember, we had quite a number of inexplicable cases of illness among the visitors – gastric cases – even typhoid . . .

KATHERINE: Yes, that's true.

DR STOCKMANN: We thought at the time they'd brought the infection with them. But when it got towards the winter – well – I began to have my doubts about it. So I set to work testing the water as well as I could . . .

KATHERINE: So that's what you were so busy doing!

DR STOCKMANN: Yes, I've been busy all right, Kate! – The trouble was I hadn't the proper laboratory apparatus – I couldn't get very far. So I sent samples of both our drinking-water and sea-water to the university for expert analysis . . .

DR HOVSTAD: And that's what's in that letter you've got there?

DR STOCKMANN (*exhibiting letter*): Yes, it's all in here! It reveals the presence of putrefying organic matter in the water – it's alive with organisms – which means it's not only dangerous to drink, but dangerous to use!

KATHERINE: What a blessing you found it out in time!

DR STOCKMANN: Yes, you may well say that, Kate.

MR HOVSTAD: Then what's your next move, Doctor?

DR STOCKMANN: Why – to put the thing right, of course.

MR HOVSTAD: I see . . . And you think that can be done?

DR STOCKMANN: It's got to be! Otherwise the whole town'll end up in hospital! As it is, the baths are ruined –

they're useless . . . But don't worry. I know exactly what's
got to be done!—

KATHERINE: But why didn't you tell us all this before, dear?

DR STOCKMANN: What – run all over the town shouting
my head off about something I wasn't sure of? No, thank
you, Kate – I'm not quite such a fool as that, y'know . . .

PETRA: Still, you might have told us here at home—

DR STOCKMANN: I couldn't tell anyone! But tomorrow, on
your way to school, you may run round and tell the
Badger—

KATHERINE: 'The Badger'! – Really, Thomas! – I've told
you before, I—

DR STOCKMANN: Well, tell your grandfather, then. It'll be a
nice surprise for the old chap – it's his tannery! He thinks
I'm not right in the upper storey – yes, and he's not the only
one, I know that! But they'll find out now, all of 'em!
(*Paces, rubbing his hands gleefully.*) What a shindy there'll be
in the town, eh, Kate! Just imagine it! All the water-pipes –
the entire system will have to be relaid!

MR HOVSTAD (*rising*): The entire system—?

DR STOCKMANN: Why, naturally. You see, the intake is too
low – it'll have to be put much higher up . . .

PETRA: So you were right, then, after all!

DR STOCKMANN: Yes – d'you remember, Petra? – I wrote
to the town clerk and pointed it out when they were
beginning to lay the foundations. But no one would take
any notice of me then! Well, I shan't wrap it up this time!
I've prepared a full and detailed report for the baths committee – in fact, it's been lying on my writing-table for over
a week now, only waiting for this to come . . . (*Flourishes
letter.*) And now they're going to have it at once! (*Crosses,
disappears into consulting-room for a moment, then returns with a
sheaf of papers.*) Here it is! My report – four closely-written
pages. – And I shall send the analysis along with it! Give me a
stiff sheet of paper to wrap it up in, Kate. – Oh anything, a

newspaper'll do . . . There – that's it! And now give it to – to
– to— (*Snaps fingers impatiently.*) Oh, what the devil's the
girl's name? – Well, give it to her anyhow, and tell her to run
round with it to the mayor!

Exit MRS STOCKMANN *by dining-room with packet.*

PETRA: What d'you think Uncle Peter'll say, Father?

DR STOCKMANN: What can he say? – He can only be grateful
to me for discovering the facts.

MR HOVSTAD: You've no objection, I take it, to our putting
a short paragraph about it in *The Herald*, Doctor?

DR STOCKMANN: No, none at all. In fact, I should be very
glad if you would.

MR HOVSTAD: Only I really do think that the sooner the
public know about it the better.

DR STOCKMANN: Yes, yes, of course.

Enter MRS STOCKMANN *by dining-room.*

KATHERINE: Well, she's just gone with it.

MR BILLING: Y'know, Doctor, this discovery of yours is
enough to make you the most important man in town – and
that's a fact!

DR STOCKMANN (*pacing – gleefully*): Nonsense! – After all,
I've only done my duty. I've made a very lucky discovery –
that's all . . . Still, all the same—

MR BILLING: Don't you think the town ought to honour
Doctor Stockmann in some way, Hovstad?

MR HOVSTAD: Yes, I certainly do. I'll put forward the
suggestion, anyhow.

MR BILLING: And I'll have a word with Aslaksen about it.

DR STOCKMANN: No. – It's very nice of you fellows – and
don't think I don't appreciate it; but I don't want any humbug of that sort. Even if the baths committee vote me an
increase in salary, I shan't accept it. No, Kate – I shan't
accept it!

KATHERINE: And I think you're quite right, Thomas!

PETRA (*raising her glass*): Good luck, Father!

MR HOVSTAD (*raising his*): Good luck, Doctor Stockmann!

MR BILLING (*doing likewise*): Good health, Doctor!

CAPT HORSTER (*clinking glasses with Dr Stockmann*): Good luck – good health – and may it bring you nothing but joy and happiness!

DR STOCKMANN: Thank you, Captain Horster . . . Thank you all – thanks, lads! I can't tell you how happy I am! Y'know, it's wonderful to feel that you've managed to be of service to your native town and your fellow-citizens! . . . Hooray, Kate! (*Seizes her round the middle and whirls her round and round, despite her laughing cries of protest. There is general laughter, applause and cheers for Dr Stockmann – and* EILIF *and* MORTEN *poke their heads round the door.*)

CURTAIN

ACT TWO

Scene – the same as Act One. The following morning. The communicating-doors to the dining-room are closed.

Enter MRS STOCKMANN *from dining-room, with a bulky envelope in her hand; she crosses to the consulting-room, opens the door and peeps in.*

KATHERINE: Are you there, Thomas?

DR STOCKMANN (*off-stage*): Yes, I've just got in. (*Enters.*) What is it, dear?

KATHERINE: A letter from Peter. (*Proffers it.*)

DR STOCKMANN (*taking it*): Let's have a look. (*Opens it and reads.*) I herewith enclose the analysis, together with your report on— (*Reads on in a low murmur.*) H'm—!

KATHERINE: What does he say, dear?

DR STOCKMANN (*thrusting envelope and contents into jacket-pocket*): Oh – he only says he's coming in to see me about midday . . .

KATHERINE: Well – see that you don't forget about it and go out again . . .

DR STOCKMANN: Oh, I shan't be going out again now – I've done this morning's round.

KATHERINE: I'm just itching to know how he'll take it . . .

DR STOCKMANN: Well – he won't be too pleased that it's I, and not he, who made the discovery . . .

KATHERINE: Yes, that's just what I'm afraid of.

DR STOCKMANN: Oh, he'll be glad enough underneath, of course; I've no doubt about that. But you know how he hates it if anyone but himself should ever do anything for the town . . .

KATHERINE: Well then, why not be generous and let him

share the credit with you? Couldn't you say it was really he who started you thinking about it in the first place – or something like that?

DR STOCKMANN: Yes, I suppose so – I don't mind. So long as I can get things put right . . .

Hall door opens a little and MORTEN KIIL *pokes his head round inquiringly, and chuckling to himself.*

MORTEN KIIL (*craftily*): Is it – is it true?

KATHERINE (*crossing to him*): Oh – it's you, Father . . .!

DR STOCKMANN: Oh, hullo, Father-in-law – good morning – come in . . .

KATHERINE: Yes, do come in, Father.

MORTEN KIIL: Ah – but only if it's true! If it's true, I'll come in – if it's not, I'm not here! – I'm off!

DR STOCKMANN: If what's true?

MORTEN KIIL: This yarn about the water-supply. Is it true?

DR STOCKMANN: Of course it is – but how did *you* hear about it?

MORTEN KIIL (*entering*): Petra looked in on her way to the school—

DR STOCKMANN: Oh, did she?

MORTEN KIIL: Ay, she told me. – I thought she was pulling my leg at first; but that's not like Petra . . .

DR STOCKMANN: Come now, surely, you don't imagine Petra'ld do a thing like that?

MORTEN KIIL: I never trust anybody; I find you can be made a fool of before you know where you are. . . . So it is true, then?

DR STOCKMANN: Yes, it's quite true, Father-in-law! Come on – sit down . . . (*Almost forces him on to sofa.*) Well now – what d'you say? – isn't it a wonderful piece of luck for the town?

MORTEN KIIL (*suppressing his laughter*): A wonderful piece of luck for the town?

DR STOCKMANN: Yes – that I discovered it in time—

MORTEN KIIL (*as before*): Ay – ay! – Only I should never have thought that you'd play such a prank on your own brother . . .

DR STOCKMANN: A prank!

KATHERINE: But, Father dear—

MORTEN KIIL (*resting his chin on his hands on the top of his stick and winking slyly at Dr Stockmann*): Let's see now – what was it again? Something about some kind of small animals that have got into the water-pipes?

DR STOCKMANN: Well, a kind of animal-life, yes – 'animal-cula' – minute organisms . . .

MORTEN KIIL: Fancy! – And quite a number of them too, according to Petra – whole swarms of them . . .

DR STOCKMANN: Yes – thousands . . . millions . . .

MORTEN KIIL: And yet no one can see 'em – is that right?

DR STOCKMANN: That's right – they're not visible to the naked eye.

MORTEN KIIL (*chuckling quietly*): Well, I'm damned if that doesn't beat cock-fighting! – It's the best one you've ever come out with!

DR STOCKMANN: What d'you mean?

MORTEN KIIL: You'll never get the mayor to swallow that one, y'know – not if you live to be a hundred!

DR STOCKMANN: Well, we shall see.

MORTEN KIIL: You don't really think he's as mad as all that, do you?

DR STOCKMANN: I hope the whole town will be.

MORTEN KIIL: The whole town! Well, you never know, it may – at that! And it'll serve 'em jolly well right! – It'll teach 'em a lesson! They think they're so much cleverer than we old ones! – Kicking me off the council like that. Yes – threw me out like a dog, that's what they did! Ah – but now it's their turn! Keep it up, Thomas! – Baste 'em! – Roast 'em!

DR STOCKMANN: But, Father-in-law, it's really—

MORTEN KIIL: Roast 'em, I say. (*Rises.*) I tell you what I'll do : if you can get the mayor and his pals to fall for it, I'll give five pounds to the poor there and then—!

DR STOCKMANN: Well, that's very nice of you—

MORTEN KIIL: And I haven't got much to throw away! – I'm not made of money! – But if you can manage that, I promise you, I'll – well, I'll give two-pounds-ten say to the poor next Christmas!

Knock on hall door, enter MR HOVSTAD.

MR HOVSTAD: Good morning. (*Pauses.*) Oh, I beg your pardon, I—

DR STOCKMANN: Oh, that's all right – come in.

MORTEN KIIL (*chuckling again*): What? Is he in it, too?

MR HOVSTAD: What d'you mean?

DR STOCKMANN: Of course he is.

MORTEN KIIL: I might have known it. Now it's going into the papers. You're a clever fellow, Thomas – and no mistake ! Well, you two do your damnedest – I'm off!

DR STOCKMANN: But you've only just come, Father-in-law !

MORTEN KIIL: I know – and I'm just going ! Do everything you can think of ! – Scare 'em into fits ! – You won't be sorry – I promise you that ! (*Crosses to hall door.*)

Exeunt MRS STOCKMANN *and* MORTEN KIIL *by hall door.*

DR STOCKMANN (*laughing*): Would you believe it? – The old chap doesn't believe a word about the water-supply.

MR HOVSTAD: Oh, so that was what he—

DR STOCKMANN: Yes, we were just talking about it. And I suppose that's what's brought you here.

MR HOVSTAD: Yes. If you've got a few moments to spare, Doctor . . .

DR STOCKMANN: Of course – as long as you like.

MR HOVSTAD: Have you heard from the mayor yet?

DR STOCKMANN: No – but he should be here shortly.

MR HOVSTAD: Well, I've been thinking a lot about this thing since last night.

DR STOCKMANN: Yes, and—?

MR HOVSTAD: As a doctor and a man of science, naturally, you see this affair of the water-supply as a perfectly clear-cut isolated issue. I don't suppose it's occurred to you that a great many other things are involved?

DR STOCKMANN: Really? – How d'you mean – Let's sit down, shall we? ... No, not there – sit here on the sofa... (MR HOVSTAD *does so. Sits in on the opposite side of table.*) Well, you think that—

MR HOVSTAD: You said yesterday that the pollution of the water is caused by various impurities in the soil.

DR STOCKMANN: Yes, there's no doubt about it – it comes from that poisonous marsh up at Molledal . . .

MR HOVSTAD: Forgive me, Doctor, but I think it's caused by a quite different sort of marsh.

DR STOCKMANN: Oh? – and what marsh is that?

MR HOVSTAD: I'm thinking of the marsh in which the whole of our municipal life is rotting!

DR STOCKMANN: Good heavens, Mr Hovstad! – What are you getting at?

MR HOVSTAD: Little by little, the affairs of this town have drifted into the hands of a pack of bureaucrats—

DR STOCKMANN: Oh come now – they're not all bureaucrats—

MR HOVSTAD: Well, not all perhaps – but those who aren't are their friends and supporters. We're completely under the thumb of a handful of wealthy men, belonging to the old families, and who've held high positions in the town for generations . . .

DR STOCKMANN: Yes, but they're also very able men, y'know—

MR HOVSTAD: They showed just how able they were when they laid the water-pipes where they did!

DR STOCKMANN: Yes, that wasn't a very clever thing to do, I admit. Still, it'll be put right soon . . .

MR HOVSTAD: D'you really think you'll get your own way so easily, then?

DR STOCKMANN: My dear man, it's common sense – it's *got* to be done!

MR HOVSTAD: Yes – but I doubt if it will be, y'know – unless the press takes it up . . .

DR STOCKMANN: I don't think even that's necessary – I'm certain my brother—

MR HOVSTAD: Well, I can assure you, Doctor, it *will* be taken up . . .

DR STOCKMANN: In your paper?

MR HOVSTAD: Yes. – You see, when I took over *The Herald*, I swore that if it was the last thing I did I'ld break up this ring of bigoted old fools, who've got us all in their grip!

DR STOCKMANN: But you told me you tried once – and nearly wrecked the paper in the process.

MR HOVSTAD: Ah, but at that time we were forced to go carefully – on account of the baths. The scheme would have fallen through, if we'd got rid of them then. But now it's an accomplished fact we can do without these expensive dignitaries.

DR STOCKMANN: Perhaps we can – but don't forget we owe them a great debt of gratitude. . . .

MR HOVSTAD: I'm not forgetting it. But, as a journalist with democratic beliefs, I can't possibly let such an opportunity slip. This myth of official infallibility must be exploded once and for all! It's a superstition that must be abolished – like any other!

DR STOCKMANN: Oh, I quite agree, Hovstad – if it's a superstition, let's have done with it!

MR HOVSTAD: I should be slow to accuse the mayor, because he's your brother. But I know you think as I do – the truth should come first. . . .

DR STOCKMANN: Yes, of course . . . (*Vehemently*.) But all the same—!

MR HOVSTAD: Now don't misunderstand me! I've no personal axe to grind in all this – I'm neither more selfish nor more ambitious than the next man . . .

DR STOCKMANN: But, my dear chap – nobody says you are . . .

MR HOVSTAD: I come of humble stock, y'know – and therefore I've had the best possible chance of learning that what the working-classes really need is to be allowed some part in the direction of public affairs, Doctor – to develop their abilities, their understanding and their self-respect—

DR STOCKMANN: Oh, I realize that all right.

MR HOVSTAD: And I feel that the journalist who allows any chance of easing the burden of the oppressed working-classes to slip through his fingers, incurs a heavy responsibility. Oh, I know perfectly well that in certain exalted circles I shall be called an agitator and so on. Well, well, they may call me what they like! – So long as my conscience is clear, I—

DR STOCKMANN: Yes, quite – quite so, Mr Hovstad. But all the same – I mean to say, hang it all—! (*Knock on hall door.*) Come in!

Enter MR ASLAKSEN. *He is poorly but neatly dressed in black, with a somewhat crumpled white cravat, a pair of well-worn gloves and a shabby-looking felt hat.*

MR ASLAKSEN (*bowing*): I hope you'll forgive me for taking the liberty, Doctor, but—

DR STOCKMANN (*rising*): Why – if it isn't Mr Aslaksen!

MR ASLAKSEN: Yes – good morning, Doctor . . .

MR HOVSTAD (*rising*): Are you looking for me, Aslaksen?

MR ASLAKSEN: No, Mr Hovstad, thank you – I didn't know you were here. I've come to see the Doctor—

DR STOCKMANN: Ah – well, and what can I do for you?

MR ASLAKSEN: Is it true – as Mr Billing tells me – that you're going to get us a new water-supply?

DR STOCKMANN: Yes, that's right – for the baths.

MR ASLAKSEN: Oh yes – yes – yes. Well then I just want to say that I'll give you all the support I possibly can.

MR HOVSTAD (*to Dr Stockmann*): There! – You see!

DR STOCKMANN: Well, that's very good of you, but—

MR ASLAKSEN: And you could do a lot worse, let me tell you, than to have us small middle-class men behind you. You see, we form what you might call a 'solid majority' in the town – when it suits us. And it's always an advantage to have the majority with you, Doctor . . .

DR STOCKMANN: Oh yes, no doubt – no doubt it is; but to be quite candid, I don't see why anything like that should be necessary in this case. After all, the thing's so clear and straightforward—

MR ASLAKSEN: All the same, it can't do any harm. Oh, I know our local authorities like the palm of my hand – they're never over-anxious to adopt suggestions coming from outside. That's why I think it might be a good thing to organize a little demonstration . . .

MR HOVSTAD: I quite agree – an excellent idea.

DR STOCKMANN: A demonstration? – But what are you going to demonstrate about?

MR ASLAKSEN: It'll be done with the greatest moderation, Doctor. I believe in moderation. Moderation – I always say – is the finest virtue a citizen can have . . .

DR STOCKMANN: Well, you're certainly well recognized for yours, Mr Aslaksen!

MR ASLAKSEN: Well – I always try to practise what I preach, Doctor. And this matter of the water-supply is very important to the small middle-class men. The baths look like being a real gold-mine for the town. We shall all benefit from them – especially householders. That's why we're so ready to support them. And, as I'm Chairman of the Householders' Association—

DR STOCKMANN: Yes—?

MR ASLAKSEN: Moreover, I'm an active member of the

Temperance Society . . . I've been a life-long advocate of
Temperance – as I expect you know, Doctor . . .

DR STOCKMANN: Yes, as a matter of fact, I do.

MR ASLAKSEN: Well, then you'll appreciate that I come into
contact with a great number of people. And, as I have the
reputation for being a moderate and law-abiding citizen – as
you yourself admitted, Doctor, I have, naturally, a certain
amount of influence in the town – even a moderate amount
of power, if I may say so.

DR STOCKMANN: Oh, I know that, Mr Aslaksen.

MR ASLAKSEN: So, you see, if it came to the point, it'ld be
the easiest thing in the world for me to arrange a little
address.

DR STOCKMANN: An address?

MR ASLAKSEN: Yes, I should call for a sort of vote of thanks
to you from the people of the town, for the prominent part
you've played in a matter of such great public importance.
Of course, it would have to be drafted in the most moderate
terms, so as not to offend the authorities and other influential people . . . But, so long as we take sufficient care
over it, I shouldn't think it'ld get anybody's back up!

MR HOVSTAD: Well, those that didn't like it would have to
lump it, that's all!

MR ASLAKSEN: No, no – no rubbing the authorities up the
wrong way, Mr Hovstad. Remember, they're in a position
to get their own back on us! – Never offend those that can
retaliate! I've done plenty of that in my time, and no good
ever came of it. But no one, of course, can take exception to
a frank, but moderate expression of a citizen's opinion . . .

DR STOCKMANN (*shaking him by the hand*): Well, my dear
Mr Aslaksen, I can't tell you how pleased I am, to find so
much support among my fellow-citizens! I'm delighted,
simply delighted! Now how about a glass of sherry?

MR ASLAKSEN: Good gracious me, no thank you, Doctor –
I never touch spirits!

DR STOCKMANN: Well, how about a nice glass of beer, then?

MR ASLAKSEN: No, nor that either, thank you, Doctor. I never touch anything in the morning! Well, I must be getting along. I want to talk to one or two householders in the town, and get to work on public opinion . . .

DR STOCKMANN: It's very kind of you, Mr Aslaksen – but I don't see that all this is really necessary, y'know . . . It seems to me that the question is a very simple and straightforward one, and—

MR ASLAKSEN: The authorities are far too fond of taking their time, Doctor. Not that I'm criticizing them for it, mind you—

MR HOVSTAD: Well, we'll give them a good shake-up in *The Herald* tomorrow, Aslaksen.

MR ASLAKSEN: Not too violently though, Mr Hovstad. You'll never get anything done if you do! – Proceed with moderation! Take my advice – I know what I'm talking about – I paid for my experience in the hard school of life, remember. Well, and now I'll say good-bye, Doctor. At least you know that you've got the small middle-class men unshakably behind you. You've the 'solid majority' on your side, Doctor!

DR STOCKMANN: That's very kind of you, Mr Aslaksen – and I very much appreciate it. (*Shakes him by the hand.*) Good-bye, good-bye.

MR ASLAKSEN: Are you coming, Mr Hovstad – I'm going past the printing-office?

MR HOVSTAD: Not just yet. I've one or two things to do first.

MR ASLAKSEN: Very well – then good-bye for the present. (*Bows and exit by hall door.*)

   DR STOCKMANN *shepherds him to the front door – then re-enters.*

MR HOVSTAD: Well, what d'you say now, Doctor? . . .

Don't you think it's about time we put an end to all this
dithering weakness and cowardice?

DR STOCKMANN: Of which Aslaksen is an example . . .?
Is that what you think?

MR HOVSTAD: Yes, I do. Oh, he's a decent enough fellow in
his own way; but he's just another stick-in-the-mud. And
most of the others are just like him – always wavering, first
on one side, then on the other; they're so chock full of doubts
and hesitations that they daren't make up their minds about
anything, let alone take any positive step!

DR STOCKMANN: Well, y'know, Aslaksen seems well-
meaning enough to me . . .

MR HOVSTAD: I dare say. But I demand more than that of a
man – he must mean well enough to act confidently on his
principles.

DR STOCKMANN: Oh, I quite agree with you.

MR HOVSTAD: That's why I'm determined to seize this
opportunity, and see if I can't infuse a little life into all these
well-meaning people for once! Worship of authority has
got to be stamped out in this town! And this criminal
blunder over the water-supply must be brought home to
every single voter in the municipality!

DR STOCKMANN: Well, if you think it's for the common
good . . . but not until I've had a word with my
brother . . .

MR HOVSTAD: All right. . . . But my leading article has still
to be written – and if the mayor refuses to take the matter
up—

DR STOCKMANN: But how could he possibly refuse—?

MR HOVSTAD: Oh, you never know, he might. And if he
does—

DR STOCKMANN: Then, I promise you – Look here, if he
does, then you may print my report – every word of it!

MR HOVSTAD: Really? – D'you mean that?

DR STOCKMANN (giving it to him): Here it is. Take it with

you. In any case, it won't do any harm for you to read it –
you can let me have it back later.

MR HOVSTAD: Good, good! – I'll do that. And now I must
be off. Good-bye, Doctor.

DR STOCKMANN: Good-bye, good-bye. (*Shepherds him to
hall door.*) It'll all be perfectly plain-sailing, Mr Hovstad –
you'll see . . . There's nothing whatever to worry about.

MR HOVSTAD: H'm – well, I hope you're right. (*Bows and
exit.*)

DR STOCKMANN (*crossing to dining-room door, opening it and
looking in – calling*): Kate! . . . Oh, so you're home, Petra?

PETRA (*entering*): Yes; we finished school early this morning.

KATHERINE (*entering*): Hasn't he been yet?

DR STOCKMANN: Peter? No – but I've been having a long
talk with Hovstad. He's quite worked up about it – Apparently, this thing's far more important than I ever imagined.
He's placed his paper at my disposal, in case I should need it.

KATHERINE: And d'you think you will, then?

DR STOCKMANN: No; I doubt it. Still, we should feel proud
to know that we've got the free, independent press on our
side. Yes, and not only that – I've just had a visit from the
Chairman of the Householders' Association?

KATHERINE: Oh? Mr Aslaksen? – and what did he want?

DR STOCKMANN: He came to offer me his support. They'll
back me up, if necessary. In fact, Kate – d'you know what
I've got behind me?

KATHERINE: No – what?

DR STOCKMANN: The 'solid majority'.

KATHERINE: Oh. . . . And is that a good thing for you,
Thomas?

DR STOCKMANN: Yes, rather! – I should just think it is!
(*Rubs his hands together and paces.*) Ah, it's a wonderful thing
to feel oneself in such brotherhood with one's fellow-
citizens!

PETRA: And to be doing so much good, Father!

DR STOCKMANN: Yes – and for one's own town, into the bargain!

KATHERINE: Wasn't that a ring at the bell?

DR STOCKMANN: I expect that's Peter. (*Knock on hall door.*) Come in!

Enter PETER STOCKMANN *from hall.*

PETER: Good morning.

DR STOCKMANN: Come in, Peter. Come in—

KATHERINE: Good morning, Peter. How are you today?

PETER: Oh, middling, thanks, Katherine. (*To Dr Stockmann.*) Yesterday evening, after office hours, I received from you a lengthy communication on the subject of the water at the baths . . .

DR STOCKMANN: That's right. – Have you read it?

PETER: I have.

DR STOCKMANN: And what d'you think about it?

PETER (*with a sideway glance*): H'm!—

KATHERINE: Come along, Petra – you can help me in the other room . . .

Exeunt MRS STOCKMANN *and* PETRA *into dining-room.*

PETER (*after a pause*): Was it necessary to make all these investigations behind my back?

DR STOCKMANN: Yes, because until I was absolutely certain, I—

PETER: You mean you are absolutely certain, then?

DR STOCKMANN: You say you've read my communication as you call it; well, surely that must have convinced you . . .

PETER: And is it your intention to bring this paper before the baths committee as a sort of official report?

DR STOCKMANN: Of course. Something must be done about it – and without any delay, either.

PETER: As usual, I notice you haven't been able to avoid the use of some pretty strong expressions in your report. For instance, among other things, you say that what we're offering our visitors is a course of slow poison!

DR STOCKMANN: Well, how would you describe it then, Peter? Just think now – poisonous water unfit for human consumption and unfit to bathe in! And this is what we offer to the poor invalids who come here in good faith and pay through the nose to be cured!

PETER: And you draw the following conclusions: that we must not only build a sewer to carry off the alleged impurities from Molledal, but re-lay all the water-pipes as well!

DR STOCKMANN: That's right. Why? D'you see any other way out of it? – because I don't.

PETER: I made an excuse to call in and have a word with the borough engineer this morning. I mentioned the matter as something we might have to think about in the future . . .

DR STOCKMANN: In the future!

PETER: Naturally, he just laughed at what he considered my extravagance. Have you, by any chance, taken the trouble to think about what your proposed alterations would cost? From what he told me, I should say somewhere between forty and fifty thousand pounds!

DR STOCKMANN: Really? – as much as all that, eh?

PETER: Yes, and that's not the worst; the job'ld take at least two years.

DR STOCKMANN: Two years! Is that really the case?

PETER: It certainly is. And what are we going to do with the baths in the meantime? We should have to close them – we should have no alternative! Besides, d'you suppose anyone would ever come near the place again, once it got round that there was something wrong with the water?

DR STOCKMANN: But there is, Peter – and you can't get away from it!

PETER: And all this has to happen now, just when the baths are beginning to pay handsomely! And we're not the only town along this coast, y'know, that lays claim to being a health-resort! Why, the others wouldn't lose a minute –

they'ld strain every muscle – to divert the full stream of
visitors to themselves! There's no doubt about that! – And
then where should we be? We'ld probably have to shut
down the baths for good – abandon the whole costly undertaking! – and all through you! You'ld have ruined your own
town!

DR STOCKMANN: I – ruined—

PETER: Of course! – Why, the town wouldn't have any
future worth mentioning if it weren't for the baths. – You
know that, as well as I do!

DR STOCKMANN: Then what d'you think ought to be
done?

PETER: I'm not yet by any means convinced that the condition of the water at the baths is as serious as you try to
make out.

DR STOCKMANN: I tell you that, if anything, it's worse! Or,
at any rate, it will be in the summer, when the hot weather
sets in.

PETER: As I said, I think you're exaggerating. And, anyhow, a
really competent medical officer ought to know what
measures to take in a case like that. He should be able to
prevent its having any harmful effect, and, if by chance it
had, he should be able to cure it!

DR STOCKMANN: Really? – Is that all?

PETER: The baths have a water-supply. That's an existing fact,
and it must be recognized as such! However, that isn't to say
that at some future date the committee would not be prepared – subject to the necessary finance being available, of
course – to consider the possibility of introducing certain
modifications . . .

DR STOCKMANN: And d'you suppose I should let myself be
implicated in a fraudulent action like that?

PETER: Fraudulent?

DR STOCKMANN: Yes, fraudulent! – It'ld be false repre-
sentation, a trick, a lie! – an absolute crime! – not only

against the public, but against the whole notion of civilized society!

PETER: As I said just now, I'm not by any means convinced yet that there is actually any imminent danger . . .

DR STOCKMANN: Oh yes, you are! – It's impossible *not* to be convinced! I presented you with a bald statement of *fact* – every word of it's true, and you know it, Peter! – only you won't acknowledge it! It was all through you that the baths and the water-pipes were built where they are! You made a blunder, and you're afraid to admit it! Pah! – D'you think I don't see through you!

PETER: And even if that were true? If I show a little concern for my reputation, it's only for the good of the town! Without moral authority I shouldn't be able to conduct affairs in the way I think best for the public good! For that reason – and for some others – it's absolutely vital to me that your report shouldn't go before the committee. In the public interest, it's simply got to be withheld! Then, later on, I shall tactfully bring the matter up for discussion, and we'll do the best we can – quietly. But not a whisper, not a hint of this unfortunate business must leak out to the public!

DR STOCKMANN: But, my dear Peter, I don't see how you're going to prevent it.

PETER: It must be prevented – it's got to be!

DR STOCKMANN: But it can't be, I tell you – too many people know about it already.

PETER: Who? – What people? – Surely not those fellows on *The Herald*?

DR STOCKMANN: Oh yes, they know. And they're the free and independent press, remember. They'll see to it that you do the right thing!

PETER (*after a slight pause*): Y'know, you're an incredibly reckless man, Thomas. I don't suppose it ever occurred to you that this may very well have serious consequences for you?

DR STOCKMANN: Serious consequences? – for me?

PETER: Yes – and for your family.

DR STOCKMANN: Just what d'you mean by that? – What are you driving at?

PETER: Correct me if I'm wrong, Thomas; but I think I'm right in saying I've always been a good brother to you. – I've always tried to lend a helping hand, and I've done what I could for you . . .

DR STOCKMANN: Yes, you have – and I'm grateful for it.

PETER: You needn't be. In a way, I had to do it as much for my own sake as for yours. You see, I thought that by helping you to improve your financial position, I should be able to keep you a little in line . . .

DR STOCKMANN: What! So it was only for your own sake!

PETER: To some extent, I say. After all, it's most embarrassing for a man holding a high civic office, to have his nearest relative behaving irresponsibly and putting his foot in it time after time . . .

DR STOCKMANN: So that's what I do, is it?

PETER: Yes, unfortunately, you do – and without even knowing it. The trouble with you is you've a restless, undisciplined and rebellious nature – coupled with a disastrous urge to rush into print about anything and everything. No sooner d'you get an idea than you've got to write a newspaper article – or even a whole pamphlet – about it!

DR STOCKMANN: But isn't it one's duty, to communicate it to the public – when one has a new idea that concerns them?

PETER: The public doesn't want any new ideas. The public's better off with the good old established ideas it's been used to.

DR STOCKMANN: And you're not ashamed to say that?

PETER: No – for once I'm being perfectly frank. So far, I've tried to avoid it, because I know how touchy you are. But now you're going to hear some home-truths, Thomas. You've no conception of the harm you do yourself poking your nose in where it's not wanted – always complaining to

the authorities and criticizing the government, telling them
they don't know their own business, shouting them down –
and then, when they pay no attention to you, insisting
you've been slighted and treated as a crank! But what else
can you expect, when you're so impossible?

DR STOCKMANN: Really! – So I'm impossible?

PETER: Yes, Thomas; and I'm afraid you're an impossible
man to work with! I know that from experience! You've
no consideration whatsoever for anybody or anything. You
seem completely to overlook the fact that you've me – and
only me – to thank for your appointment as medical officer
to the baths. . . .

DR STOCKMANN: You to thank! – It was mine by right! –
No one else was entitled to it! It was actually I who discovered the town's potentialities as a health-resort! No one
else ever had the idea! Why, for years I fought for it single-
handed, I wrote and wrote—

PETER: I'm not saying you didn't; but it wasn't the right time
for it then – though you weren't to know that in your
remote little world up north. But, as soon as the opportune
moment arrived, I – and others – took the matter up and—

DR STOCKMANN: Yes – and made a thorough mess of it –
completely disregarded my careful plan, and ruined the
whole thing! Well, we can see now what a bunch of
geniuses you were!

PETER: You're simply finding a pretext for your usual
hostility – attacking your superiors – it's an old habit of
yours! You can't stand authority – you just can't take orders,
you never could! You look down on anyone who holds a
higher position than you – you regard him as a personal
enemy; and any brick's good enough to throw at him!
However, I've tried my utmost to make it plain to you just
how much is at stake for the town – and, necessarily for me,
too. And therefore, Thomas, you'll find me absolutely
adamant about what I'm going to ask you to do now!

DR STOCKMANN: Really? – And what's that?

PETER: Well, as you haven't had sense enough to keep your mouth shut about this extremely delicate matter, which should, in any case, have been treated officially as highly confidential, it's obviously too late now to attempt to hush it up in any way. All sorts of rumours'll be going around before very long; and no doubt they'll be embroidered by our enemies. So there's only one thing you can do – and that's publicly to contradict them!

DR STOCKMANN: I? – How? – I don't understand—

PETER: Oh, it's quite simple. We shall expect you to state that, after further investigations, you've come to the conclusion that the matter is after all by no means as serious or urgent as you had at first thought. . . .

DR STOCKMANN: Oho! – You expect me to do that – do you?

PETER: —And, of course, to express your complete confidence in the committee and in their willingness to carry out, thoroughly and conscientiously, whatever measures they consider necessary to remedy any possible defects . . .

DR STOCKMANN: But you'll never be able to do that by tinkering about and patching it up – it's a job that's got to be done properly. I'm serious about it, Peter. – It's my absolute conviction that—

PETER (interrupting him): As a servant of the committee you've no right to any personal convictions . . . !

DR STOCKMANN (almost dumbfounded): No right to—?

PETER: —Not in your official capacity. As a private individual, of course, it's quite another matter. But as a subordinate official on the staff of the baths, you've no right to express a conviction that conflicts with that of your superiors!

DR STOCKMANN: This is too much! I, a doctor, a man of science, have no right to—!

PETER: This matter is not purely a scientific one. It's extremely complicated – there's not only a financial side to it, but a technical one as well, remember.

DR STOCKMANN: I don't care a damn what there is! Nothing's going to stop me from speaking my mind on any subject under the sun!

PETER: That's your business – so long as it has nothing to do with the baths. That – surely you can see we must forbid?

DR STOCKMANN (*shouting*): You forbid—! You! A gang of—

PETER: Yes, forbid it. – *I*, as chairman of the committee and your employer, forbid it! And if I forbid it, you have to obey!

DR STOCKMANN (*controlling himself*): Peter, if you weren't my brother—

Dining-room door is thrown open and enter PETRA.

PETRA: Father! – Don't you stand that!

Enter MRS STOCKMANN *from dining-room.*

KATHERINE: Petra! – Petra!

PETER: Oh, so we've been eavesdropping, have we?

KATHERINE: You were both shouting so loud, we could hardly help—

PETRA: Yes, I *was* listening – I listened on purpose!

PETER: Well, in a way I'm not altogether sorry—

DR STOCKMANN (*approaching him*): Well, go on – what were you saying about forbidding and obeying—?

PETER: You forced me to adopt that tone.

DR STOCKMANN: So I'm to call myself a liar in public, is that it?

PETER: We consider it essential that you should make a public statement on the lines I've indicated.

DR STOCKMANN: And if I don't do as I'm told – what then?

PETER: Then we shall issue a statement ourselves to reassure the public.

DR STOCKMANN: Very well, I can write too, y'know! – I'll stick to my guns, and I'll prove that I'm right and you're wrong! And what'll you do then?

PETER: Then I shall be powerless to prevent your dismissal!

DR STOCKMANN: What—!

PETRA: Father! – Dismissal!

KATHERINE: Dismissal!

PETER: Your dismissal as medical officer to the baths. I shall be faced with no alternative but to propose that you shall be given instant notice and shall have no further connection whatever with the baths.

DR STOCKMANN: And you'ld dare to do that!

PETER: It's you who are daring – allowing yourself to go to such lengths!

PETRA: Uncle, this is a shocking way to treat a man like Father!

KATHERINE: Oh, do be quiet, Petra!

PETER (*looking at Petra*): Oh, so we've got opinions of our own already, have we? Well, I'm not surprised. (*To Mrs Stockmann.*) Katherine – you appear to be about the most level-headed person in this house. Use whatever influence you may have with your husband, and try to make him see what all this means both for his family—

DR STOCKMANN: My family's my own affair – and nobody else's!

PETER: I was saying – both for his family and for the town he lives in.

DR STOCKMANN: I'm the one that really cares about the town! I want to expose a disgraceful state of affairs that sooner or later must come out! Oh, you'll see whether I love my own town!

PETER: That's why you're trying so hard to cut off the town's main source of revenue, I suppose?

DR STOCKMANN: But don't you understand? – the source is poisoned, man! Are you mad? We're a health-resort – and we're selling dirt and disease! Why, the whole of our flourishing social life's founded on a lie!

PETER: Sheer imagination, or even worse! The man who

can make such vile suggestions about his own town is
nothing but an enemy of the people!

DR STOCKMANN (*going up to him*): You dare to—!

KATHERINE (*throwing herself between them*): Thomas!

PETRA (*seizing his arm*): Don't lose your temper, Father!

PETER: I'm not staying here to expose myself to physical
violence! You've had your warning – so just you think
about what you owe to yourself and your family! Good-
bye! (*Exit by hall door.*)

DR STOCKMANN (*pacing*): And I have to put up with treat-
ment like that! And in my own home too, Kate! – What do
you think about it? – eh?

KATHERINE: I think it's a shame and a disgrace, really,
Thomas. . . .

PETRA: Oh, how I should love to give Uncle a piece of my
mind—!

DR STOCKMANN: It's all my own fault – I ought to have
stood up to him years ago – shown my teeth! – and bitten!
And then to be called an enemy of the people! Me ! Good
God – I'm not going to stand that!

KATHERINE: But Thomas dear, when all's said and done your
brother has got the power—

DR STOCKMANN: Yes – but I have the right, Kate—!

KATHERINE: Yes – yes – the right.... But what's the good of
that if you haven't any 'might'?

PETRA: Oh, Mother – how can you talk like that?

DR STOCKMANN: D'you mean to say that in a free country
like ours, there's no point in being in the right? You're
crazy, Kate! Besides, haven't I got the free, independent
press in front of me, and the 'solid majority' behind me?
That's might enough, I should think!

KATHERINE: But, good heavens, Thomas, surely you don't
intend to—?

DR STOCKMANN: Intend to what?

KATHERINE: —to set yourself against your brother . . .

DR STOCKMANN: For heaven's sake, Kate, what else d'you
expect me to do, if not to stand up for what's right and for
the truth?

PETRA: That's what *I* say!

KATHERINE: But what good will you do? – If they won't,
they won't!

DR STOCKMANN: Ho-ho, just you wait and see, Kate! – If
they want war they can have it! – I'll fight to the bitter end!

KATHERINE: Oh yes, you'll fight to the bitter end – and
you'll fight yourself out of your job, that's what you'll do!

DR STOCKMANN: Then at least I shall have done my duty to
the public, to the town! Enemy of the people, indeed! – I'll
show him!

KATHERINE: But to your family, Thomas – to us at home?
D'you think that's doing your duty to those that depend on
you?

PETRA: Ah Mother, why must you always put us first?

KATHERINE: Oh, it's easy enough for you to talk, you can
look after yourself if necessary . . . But think of the boys,
Thomas – and of yourself a little too, and of me—

DR STOCKMANN: You must be out of your mind, Kate, if
you think I'm going to be such a miserable coward as to
truckle to Peter and his precious cronies! Why, I should
never know a moment's peace for the rest of my life!

KATHERINE: Oh, I don't know anything about that – but
goodness knows what sort of life we shall all have if you go
on defying them. There you'll be again with no salary, no
regular income; and you know we've nothing else to live
on! I should have thought you'd had enough of living from
hand to mouth in the old days. Remember what they were
like, Thomas – just think what it'll mean . . . !

DR STOCKMANN (*struggling with himself and clenching his fists*):
And this is what bureaucracy can do to a decent, honest
man! It's almost incredible, isn't it, Kate?

KATHERINE: Oh – it's certainly disgraceful the way they're

treating you, there's no getting away from that. But then there's so much injustice one has to put up with in this world! There are the boys now, Thomas. Look at them. What's to become of them? Oh no, no, you can't . . . you can't possibly—

Enter EILIF *and* MORTEN *from hall, carrying their school-books.*

DR STOCKMANN: The boys . . .! (*Suddenly – firmly and decisively.*) No – never! If it's the last thing I do, I'll never bow down to this! (*Crosses to consulting-room.*)

KATHERINE (*following him*): Thomas – what are you going to do?

DR STOCKMANN (*in doorway*): I want to be able to look my boys in the face when they're grown men! (*Exit.*)

KATHERINE (*bursting into tears*): Oh, God – God help us . . .!

PETRA: Father's true as steel! – He'll never give in!

EILIF *and* MORTEN *look inquiringly and as though about to speak, but* PETRA *signals them not to.*

CURTAIN

ACT THREE

The Editor's room at The Herald *office. Left-back, the entrance door; right-back, a glass-paned door leads to the printing-office; and, down-right, another leads to the rest of the offices. Centre, a large table, littered with papers, piles of newspapers, books, proofs, etc. Down-left, a window with a desk and a high stool in front of it. A couple of arm-chairs by the table, and high-back ones here and there against the walls. The room is dingy and cheerless, the appointments shabby and the chairs stained and torn. In the printing-room can be seen compositors at work and a printer operating a hand-press.*

MR HOVSTAD *is sitting at the desk writing. After a few moments, enter* MR BILLING *by door right, with Dr Stockmann's manuscript.*

MR BILLING: Well, I must say—!

MR HOVSTAD *(still writing)*: Have you read it all?

MR BILLING *(putting ms on desk)*: Yes, I certainly have!

MR HOVSTAD: Don't you think our Doctor's a pretty hard hitter?

MR BILLING: Pretty hard? – He is – and that's a fact! Why, every word falls like – like a sledge-hammer!

MR HOVSTAD: Yes – but it'll take far more than that, y'know, to knock these fellows out.

MR BILLING: That's true – we shall simply have to keep on battering them till they collapse, that's all. . . . D'you know, as I sat in there reading that article, I could almost hear the first faint rumblings of revolution!

MR HOVSTAD *(turning round)*: Sssh! For goodness' sake don't let Aslaksen hear you talking like that!

MR BILLING *(sotto voce)*: Aslaksen! There's a coward, if you

46

like! That fellow's got about as much manhood as a worm!
But you're going to get your own way this time, aren't you?
– You *are* going to print the article?

MR HOVSTAD: Yes – unless, of course, the Mayor gives way—

MR BILLING: Now that *would* be a nuisance, wouldn't it?

MR HOVSTAD: Well, luckily we can make the most of the
situation, either way. If the Mayor won't accept Doctor
Stockmann's proposals, he'll have all the small middle-class
men down on him like a ton of bricks – the entire Householders' Association and all the rest of 'em! And if he does
accept them, he'll fall foul of all the big shareholders in the
baths, who up to now have been his strongest supporters . . .

MR BILLING: Yes – my goodness, yes! – Because, of course,
they'll have to part with quite a lot of money—

MR HOVSTAD: You bet your life they will! And then, once
the ring's broken, we'll get to work and show the public
every day just how incompetent the Mayor is! – and, of
course, keep on insisting that, for the future, the town
council – indeed, *every* responsible position – must be filled
by men of more liberal ideas.

MR BILLING: And that's the absolute truth! – every word of
it – and that's a fact! I can see it – I can see it – we're on the
eve of revolution!

Knock on entrance door.

MR HOVSTAD: Sssh! (*Calls.*) Come in! (*Entrance door opens
and enter* DR STOCKMANN. *Crosses to him.*) Ah – Doctor
Stockmann! . . . Well?

DR STOCKMANN: You may go to press, Mr Hovstad!

MR HOVSTAD: So it's come to that, has it?

MR BILLING: Hooray!

DR STOCKMANN: Yes, you may go to press. It certainly has
come to that. And if that's what they want, they shall have
it! It's open war, Mr Billing!

MR BILLING: War to the knife! – War to the death – eh,
Doctor!

DR STOCKMANN: This article's only the beginning. I've four or five others in my head already. Where's Aslaksen?

MR BILLING (*calling into printing-office*): Mr Aslaksen – just come in here for a minute, will you!

MR HOVSTAD: Four or five more? On the same subject?

DR STOCKMANN: Oh, good heavens no, my dear fellow – on all kinds of things. But they all tie up with the water-supply and the drainage question. You know how one thing leads to another – it's not unlike altering an old house—

MR BILLING: It certainly is – and that's a fact! And, before you know where you are, you find that practically the whole place has got to be pulled down!

Enter MR ASLAKSEN *from printing-office.*

MR ASLAKSEN: Pulled down? Surely the Doctor isn't going to pull down the baths?

MR HOVSTAD: No, nothing like that – you needn't be alarmed.

DR STOCKMANN: We were talking about something quite different. Well, and what d'you think of the article, Mr Hovstad?

MR HOVSTAD: I think it's an absolute masterpiece . . . !

DR STOCKMANN: Good – I'm glad. I don't think too badly of it myself!

MR HOVSTAD: It's so clear and concise and it doesn't mince matters. And one hasn't to be an expert to understand it, that's what I like! You'll have every thinking person on your side, once they've read it!

DR STOCKMANN: And every prudent one too, I hope!

MR BILLING: And the imprudent ones as well – almost the whole population, I shouldn't wonder . . .

MR ASLAKSEN: In that case, I should think, we may venture to print it.

DR STOCKMANN: So I should think!

MR HOVSTAD: It'll go in tomorrow.

DR STOCKMANN: I'm glad to hear it – because we've no time

to lose, y'know! Mr Aslaksen I want you to do something for me: could you supervise the setting-up of my article yourself?

MR ASLAKSEN: Yes – certainly I will, Doctor.

DR STOCKMANN: And take the greatest possible care over it – no misprints, mind – every word's important! I'll look in later; and perhaps you'll be able to let me see a galley-proof. I can't tell you how anxious I am to see the thing in print, to see it fired off—

MR BILLING: Yes – like a bombshell!

DR STOCKMANN: —and presented for consideration by every intelligent citizen. Oh, you've no idea what I've had to submit to today. – I've been threatened with practically everything; they even tried to deprive me of my normal rights as a human being—

MR BILLING: What? They tried that?

DR STOCKMANN: Yes – I was expected to humble myself – grovel to expediency – and put my personal advantage above my deepest convictions—

MR BILLING: Absolutely outrageous – and that's a fact!

MR HOVSTAD: What else can you expect from that crowd?

DR STOCKMANN: Well – they'll find they picked the wrong man – and they'll find it right away, in black and white. I'll see to that! From now on *The Herald* shall be my artillery. – I'll bombard them with one article after another—

MR ASLAKSEN: Yes, but look here—

MR BILLING: Hooray! It's war – war!

DR STOCKMANN: I shall batter down their defences and crush them and expose them in the eyes of all decent-minded people! – That's what I shall do!

MR ASLAKSEN: Yes, but with moderation, Doctor – it must be done with moderation—

MR BILLING: What's the good of that? – Don't spare the dynamite, I say!

DR STOCKMANN: —Because it's no longer merely a question

of the water-supply and drainage, y'know. – It's the whole of
our public life that's got to be decontaminated – disin-
fected . . .

MR BILLING: That's the voice of salvation! – That's . . . !

DR STOCKMANN: All the old bunglers must go! – *all* of
'em – in every cosy official nook! I've seen so far ahead
today that it's still all a little blurred – but I shall see it clearly
soon. We must look around us for new young blood,
doughty standard-bearers – resolute captains for the outposts - that's what we need!

MR BILLING: Hear, hear!

DR STOCKMANN: And, if only we stand together, it'll be
easy! Our so-called revolution'll be launched as smoothly
as an ocean liner. Don't you think so?

MR HOVSTAD: Personally, I think we've every chance now
of getting municipal control into the right hands at last!

MR ASLAKSEN: And, so long as we do everything with
moderation, I really don't see that there can be any danger . . .

DR STOCKMANN: Who the devil cares about danger? What
I do, I do in the name of truth and for my conscience sake.

MR HOVSTAD: Well, you most certainly deserve all the
support you can get, Doctor.

MR ASLAKSEN: Yes, there's no doubt about it, the Doctor's a
true friend of the town – in fact, a real friend of the community.

MR BILLING: Doctor Stockmann's a friend of the *people*,
Mr Aslaksen – and that's a fact!

MR ASLAKSEN: A friend of the people – yes . . . Now I come
to think of it, that'ld be rather a good phrase for the Householders' Association to adopt.

DR STOCKMANN (*touched; grasping their hands*): Thanks,
thanks friends – it does me good to hear you! My brother
the Mayor called me something very different. But I'll pay
him back all right! And now I must be getting along. I've
got a patient to see. I'll be back shortly. Be careful with that

article, Aslaksen – and don't leave out any of the exclamation marks – add a few more if you want to! Well, good-bye for the present – good-bye, good-bye.

OMNES *shepherd him to entrance door and exit* DR STOCK-MANN.

MR HOVSTAD: He'll be worth his weight in gold to us, that man!

MR ASLAKSEN: Yes, so long as he confines himself to this matter of the baths. But if he goes beyond that then I think we should be very ill-advised to follow him . . .

MR HOVSTAD: H'm – that of course depends on—

MR BILLING: You're always so damned scared of things, Aslaksen!

MR ASLAKSEN: Scared? Well, I may be a trifle cautious when it comes to the local authorities, Mr Billing. – I learnt that in the hard school of experience, let me tell you. But try me in high politics – put me up against the government itself, and then see if I'm scared!

MR BILLING: No, you're not – and that's where you're so inconsistent.

MR ASLAKSEN: I have a very strong sense of what is practical – that's all. You can attack the government as much as you like, without doing anybody any harm; because, you see, politicians don't care – they know that once they're in, they're in. But local authorities *can* be turned out, and then you might get an even more ignorant lot in, who'll do goodness knows what harm to the householders and everyone else . . .

MR HOVSTAD: But what about the progressive education of the citizen in civic responsibilities? – or d'you never think of that?

MR ASLAKSEN: When a man has solid interests to protect, he can't think of everything, Mr Hovstad.

MR HOVSTAD: Then I hope I shall never have any solid interests to protect!

MR BILLING: Hear, hear!

MR ASLAKSEN (*smiling*): H'm! (*Points to desk.*) Don't forget that Mr Stensgard, who sat in that chair before you, is now an alderman . . .

MR BILLING (*spitting*): Pah! – That turncoat!

MR HOVSTAD: I'm no weathercock – and I never will be!

MR ASLAKSEN: A politician should never be too sure of anything, Mr Hovstad. And as for you, Mr Billing, I should be a little more moderate, if I were you, seeing that you've applied for the post of general secretary to the town council!

MR BILLING: I—!

MR HOVSTAD: Have you, Billing?

MR BILLING: Well, yes – I have, I suppose; but only to annoy them – just to see if I can't take them down a peg or two, if you know what I mean . . .

MR ASLAKSEN: Anyhow, that's got nothing to do with me. But if I'm to be accused of inconsistency and cowardice, I should just like to point out that my political past's an open book; and if I have changed at all through the years it's only to favour greater moderation. Although my heart's with the man in the street, I have got a little sympathy for the authorities – the local ones, I mean. . . . (*Exit into printing-office.*)

MR BILLING: Don't you think it's about time we tried to get rid of him, Hovstad?

MR HOVSTAD: D'you know anyone else who'll foot our paper and printing bills?

MR BILLING: It's a damned nuisance being without capital!

MR HOVSTAD: Yes, if only we'd got that!

MR BILLING: How about approaching Doctor Stockmann?

MR HOVSTAD (*turning over papers*): What's the point? – He hasn't got any money.

MR BILLING: No, but he's got his father-in-law, old Morten Kiil – 'The Badger', as they call him – behind him.

MR HOVSTAD (*writing*): And what makes you so sure *he's* got any.

MR BILLING: Oh – there's plenty of money there! And some of it's bound to go to the Stockmann family. He's sure to provide for – for the children at any rate.

MR HOVSTAD (*half-turning*): Is that what you're counting on?

MR BILLING: Counting on? I never count on anything.

MR HOVSTAD: Quite right too! And I shouldn't count on that secretaryship either, if I were you – because I can assure you you won't get it.

MR BILLING: D'you think I don't know that? As a matter of fact, that's just what I want. I only applied for it out of sheer cussedness. That sort of slap puts new fight into you – gives you a fresh supply of venom. – And that's just what you need in a godforsaken hole like this, where nothing exciting ever happens!

MR HOVSTAD (*writing*): Yes . . . may be . . .

MR BILLING: Well, they'll hear from me now all right! – I'm going in to write the appeal to the Householders' Association! (*Exit by door right.*)

MR HOVSTAD (*sitting at desk, biting his penholder; slowly*): H'm – so that's it, is it?—(*Knock on entrance door.*) Come in! (*Enter* PETRA STOCKMANN. *Rises.*) Why, it's you! –Well, this is a pleasant surprise!

PETRA: Oh, I do hope I'm not—

MR HOVSTAD (*offering her chair*): Good heavens, no. Come in – sit down . . .

PETRA: No, thanks – I really haven't time, I only looked in for a moment.

MR HOVSTAD: I see. – Something to do with your father?

PETRA: No; as a matter of fact, it's to do with me. (*Takes out a book from pocket.*) Here's that story back.

MR HOVSTAD: Why? – what's wrong?

PETRA: I'm sorry but I can't possibly translate *that*!

MR HOVSTAD: But you promised—

PETRA: Yes, I know; but, as you see, I hadn't read it then. I don't suppose you've read it either?

MR HOVSTAD: No, of course, I haven't – you know I don't know English. But—

PETRA: Exactly – and that's why I've come to tell you that you must find something else to put in. (*Puts book on table.*) You can't possibly use this in *The Herald.*

MR HOVSTAD: Oh? – Why not?

PETRA: Because it simply contradicts all your own principles.

MR HOVSTAD: Well, for that matter—

PETRA: But you don't understand. – It takes the view that there's a kindly Providence which looks after the so-called good people in this world, and turns everything to their advantage, while all the so-called bad people are punished…!

MR HOVSTAD: Well, and what's wrong with that? – That's just the sort of thing the public likes!

PETRA: And d'you mean to say you'ld give it to them? You don't believe a word of it yourself. – You know perfectly well that things don't happen like that in real life!

MR HOVSTAD: Of course they don't – but an editor can't always do as he likes, y'know. He's got to indulge people's weaknesses some of the time, especially in trifles. After all, the important thing is politics – at any rate for a newspaper; and if I want people to follow me along the path of progress towards freedom, I mustn't scare them away. If they find a nice serial story with a moral at the bottom of the page, they'll be all the more ready to cast a friendly eye over what's at the top. – It creates confidence!

PETRA: You ought to be ashamed of yourself! I'd no idea you were such a hypocrite! Fancy tricking people like that! You're worse than a spider!

MR HOVSTAD (*smiling*): Thank you for having such a high opinion of me! No; actually, the idea was Billing's, not mine …

PETRA: Mr Billing's!

MR HOVSTAD: Yes – at least he came out with it the other day. It's he who's so anxious to run it as a serial, I'd never even heard of the book.

PETRA: But how on earth can Mr Billing with his advanced views—

MR HOVSTAD: Well, you see, Billing's a man of many parts. Now, I hear, he's applying for the post as secretary to the town council.

PETRA: I don't believe it, Mr Hovstad. How could he possibly sink so low as that!

MR HOVSTAD: Well, you could always ask him.

PETRA: I'ld never have thought it of him!

MR HOVSTAD (*looking at her more closely*): Why? Is it such a very great surprise to you, then?

PETRA: Yes – or perhaps not altogether. Oh – I don't know, really . . .

MR HOVSTAD: We journalists aren't worth very much, y'know, Miss Petra.

PETRA: D'you really mean that?

MR HOVSTAD: Yes, I do – on the whole.

PETRA: Oh, in ordinary, trivial, everyday things, perhaps – I can understand that. But now that you're backing a really great cause—

MR HOVSTAD: This discovery of your father's, you mean?

PETRA: Yes, of course. I should think that ought to make you feel worth more than most people.

MR HOVSTAD: Well, curiously enough, I do feel just a little like that today . . .

PETRA: Of course you do – you must do. Oh, it's a glorious profession to be in! To blaze the way for truth and for brave new ideas! If it were no more than taking up the cudgels for a man who's been wronged—

MR HOVSTAD: Especially when that wronged man is – well, I don't quite know how to put it—

PETRA: Is so upright and completely honest, you mean?

MR HOVSTAD (*quietly*): No, I mean – especially when he's your father . . .

PETRA (*taken aback*): What?

MR HOVSTAD: Yes, Petra – Miss Petra.

PETRA: So that's what's at the back of it all? – that's what you're thinking of? – Not the cause itself? – Not the truth? – Not my father's loyalty to his fellow-creatures—?

MR HOVSTAD: Oh yes, that as well, of course.

PETRA: No, thank you, you've said quite enough already. Now I shall never, never be able to trust you again!

MR HOVSTAD: Can you really hold it against me simply because it's mostly for your sake—

PETRA: I'm holding it against you simply because you've deceived my father. You've talked to him as though the truth and the general good were all you cared about. You've been pretty heartless with both of us. You're not the man you pretended to be, Mr Hovstad. I shall never forgive you for that – never!

MR HOVSTAD: You really shouldn't be so bitter Miss Petra – least of all now, y'know.

PETRA: And why not now?

MR HOVSTAD: Because your father can't do without my help.

PETRA (*looking him up and down*): So you're even capable of that too? Aren't you ashamed?

MR HOVSTAD: I – I'm sorry, I wasn't thinking what I was saying. Please – please believe me—

PETRA: Oh, I know what to believe all right! Good-bye.

Enter MR ASLAKSEN *hurriedly from printing-office and looking somewhat mystified.*

MR ASLAKSEN: Hovstad, you'll never— (*Sees Petra.*) Oh dear – that's awkward—

PETRA: Well, there's your book. You'll have to find someone else to give it to! (*Crosses to entrance door.*)

MR HOVSTAD (*following her*): But, Miss Petra—

PETRA: Good-bye. (*Exit.*)

MR ASLAKSEN: Mr Hovstad, quick—!

MR HOVSTAD: Well, what is it?

MR ASLAKSEN: The Mayor – he's outside in the printing-office—

MR HOVSTAD: The Mayor?

MR ASLAKSEN: Yes. He wants to speak to you. He came in the back way – he didn't want to be seen . . .

MR HOVSTAD: Now I wonder what *he* wants . . . No, you stay here, I'll go myself. (*Crosses to printing-room, opens door and ushers in Peter Stockmann with a bow.*) And, Aslaksen – keep a lookout – see that nobody—

MR ASLAKSEN: Leave it to me. (*Crosses to printing-room and exits.*)

PETER: You didn't expect to see me here, Mr Hovstad.

MR HOVSTAD: No, I can't say I did.

PETER (*looking about*): Nice quarters you've got here – all very comfortable, I must say.

MR HOVSTAD: Oh—

PETER: And here am I – practically forcing my way in – to keep you from your work!

MR HOVSTAD: Oh, that's quite all right, Mr Mayor – I'm at your service. Let me take your hat and stick. (*Does so and puts them on chair.*) And please sit down – won't you?

PETER (*sitting by table*): Thank you. (MR HOVSTAD *sits.*) I've had a very trying time this morning, Mr Hovstad. . . .

MR HOVSTAD: Really? – Well, I suppose with all the various things you have to see to—

PETER: I'm sorry to say my brother – the medical officer for health – was the cause of it.

MR HOVSTAD: Really? – The Doctor?

PETER: Yes – apparently he's written some kind of report about some highly theoretical defects in the baths, which he wants placed before the committee . . .

MR HOVSTAD: Has he really?

PETER: Yes, didn't he tell you? – I'm almost sure he said—

MR HOVSTAD: Oh yes, of course, I believe he did say something about—

    Enter MR ASLAKSEN *from printing-office.*

MR ASLAKSEN: You forgot to give me the article, I—

MR HOVSTAD (*irritably*): Ach! – there it is over there on the desk!

MR ASLAKSEN (*taking it*): Ah yes, so it is. Thank you.

PETER: Why, those papers – that's the very thing I was—

MR ASLAKSEN: It's an article by Doctor Stockmann, your worship.

MR HOVSTAD: Oh, is that what you were referring to?

PETER: Yes, that's it. What d'you think of it?

MR HOVSTAD: Well, I'm not a very technically-minded person, I've really scarcely glanced at it . . .

PETER: But you are going to print it!

MR HOVSTAD: I can hardly refuse a signed article by so distinguished a—

MR ASLAKSEN: It's nothing to do with me, Mr Mayor – *I've* nothing to do with what goes into the paper . . .

PETER: No, no, of course not.

MR ASLAKSEN: I just print what I'm given.

PETER: Naturally, of course.

MR ASLAKSEN: So, if you don't mind, I'll— (*Crosses to printing-office.*)

PETER: Just a moment, Mr Aslaksen. With your permission, Mr Hovstad—

MR HOVSTAD: By all means, your worship.

PETER: Now you're a sensible and level-headed man, Mr Aslaksen. . . .

MR ASLAKSEN: I'm glad you think so, Mr Mayor.

PETER: And one of very wide influence, too.

MR ASLAKSEN: Well – chiefly among the small middle-class men, y'know—

PETER: The small ratepayers form the majority here – as everywhere else.

MR ASLAKSEN: That's true, your worship.

PETER: And I've no doubt you know how they feel about most things. – Isn't that so?

MR ASLAKSEN: Yes, I think I may say I do.

PETER: Well – I must say, I think such unselfish willingness on the part of the town's poorer classes to make further sacrifices like this—

MR ASLAKSEN: What? – I—

MR HOVSTAD: Sacrifices?

PETER: It's most heartening evidence of public spirit and goodwill – most heartening. It's certainly far more than I ever expected. But then, of course, you're in much closer touch with public opinion than I am.

MR ASLAKSEN: Yes, but, your worship . . .

PETER: And it's by no means a small sacrifice the town will have to make.

MR HOVSTAD: The town?

MR ASLAKSEN: But I don't understand. Surely the baths—

PETER: At a very rough estimate the alterations proposed by the Doctor will cost something like forty thousand pounds.

MR ASLAKSEN: That's a lot of money, but—

PETER: Naturally, we shall have to raise a municipal loan.

MR HOVSTAD (rising): You're surely not suggesting that the town—?

MR ASLAKSEN: You don't mean to say that it's got to come out of the rates? – Out of the pockets of the small middle-class men? Why, that'ld mean another increase!

PETER: But, my dear Mr Aslaksen, where else is the money to come from?

MR ASLAKSEN: That's a matter for the owners of the baths – they'll have to find it!

PETER: But the proprietors of the baths are not in a position to incur any further expense, I'm afraid.

MR HOVSTAD: Are you quite sure of that, Mr Mayor?

PETER: Yes, I've made it my business to find out. If the town wants these very extensive alterations carried out, then the town will have to shoulder the cost.

MR ASLAKSEN: But damn it all! – I beg your pardon! – This is quite another matter, Mr Hovstad.

MR HOVSTAD: Yes, it certainly is.

PETER: And, to make matters worse, we shall have to close the baths for about two years.

MR HOVSTAD: Close them? – What – altogether?

MR ASLAKSEN: For two years?

PETER: Yes, the work'll take at least that time.

MR ASLAKSEN: But, damn it all, we can't have that, your worship! What are we householders going to live on in the meantime?

PETER: That, unfortunately, isn't easy to say, Mr Aslaksen. But what else can we do? D'you suppose a single visitor will come here if we start putting the idea into people's heads that our water's polluted, that the place is a source of infection, that the entire town—

MR ASLAKSEN: Is that all it is, then? – just an idea?

PETER: With the best will in the world, I haven't been able to convince myself that it's anything else.

MR ASLAKSEN: Well then, in that case, I think it's unforgivable of Doctor Stockmann – Oh, I beg your pardon, Mr Mayor, but—

PETER: What you say is only too true, I'm afraid, Mr Aslaksen. My brother, I regret to say, has always been rather impulsive . . .

MR ASLAKSEN: And d'you still intend to support him in this, Mr Hovstad?

MR HOVSTAD: How was I to know that—?

PETER: Anyhow, I've drawn up a short statement of the facts as I'm sure they would appear to any reasonable person; and in it I've shown how any possible defects could perfectly well be put right without any great loss of revenue, and within the present financial capacity of the baths. . . .

MR HOVSTAD: Have you got it with you, your worship?

PETER (*feeling in his pocket*): Yes – I brought it with me in case you—

MR ASLAKSEN (*quickly*): Oh – good heavens! – There he is!

PETER: Who? – My brother?

MR HOVSTAD: Where? – Where is he?

MR ASLAKSEN: He's just come in the side door – he's coming through the printing-office . . .

PETER: Then he'd better not find me here! A pity – There are still several things I want to talk to you about.

MR HOVSTAD (*pointing to door right*): Then go in there for a moment . . .

PETER: But—?

MR HOVSTAD: It's all right – no one's there – only Billing.

MR ASLAKSEN: Hurry, your worship – he's just coming!

PETER: Very well, then – but get rid of him as quickly as you can! (*Exit by door right, which* MR ASLAKSEN *opens for him and closes behind him.*)

MR HOVSTAD: Pretend to be doing something, Aslaksen. (*Sits at desk and writes.*)

MR ASLAKSEN *turns to a pile of newspapers on a chair, and begins to look through them, as enter* DR STOCKMANN *from printing-office.*

DR STOCKMANN (*putting down hat and stick*): Ah well – here we are again!

MR HOVSTAD (*writing*): What, are you back already, Doctor? . . . Hurry up with whatever it is, Aslaksen – we've a lot to do today, y'know.

DR STOCKMANN: No proofs yet, I hear.

MR ASLAKSEN (*without turning round*): No – you could hardly expect them in that time, Doctor.

DR STOCKMANN: No, I suppose not. – I can't help being a

little impatient, that's all. I shan't get a moment's peace till I
see it in print!

MR HOVSTAD: H'm – it'll take some time yet, won't it,
Aslaksen?

MR ASLAKSEN: Yes, I'm afraid it will.

DR STOCKMANN: All right then, I'll look in again. I don't
mind coming back twice if necessary – it's so important.
After all, what's a little shoe-leather compared with the
welfare of the town! (*Is about to go, but stops and turns.*) Oh,
but there's just one other thing!—

MR HOVSTAD: Couldn't we leave it till some other time,
Doctor, I—?

DR STOCKMANN: Oh, it won't take a moment. It's only
this: when people open their papers tomorrow and read my
article, and discover that I've been quietly working for the
good of the town all winter—

MR HOVSTAD: Yes, but, Doctor—

DR STOCKMANN: I know what you're going to say— It was
no more than my duty – my plain duty as a citizen. Of
course, I know that as well as you do. But, you see, it's my
fellow-citizens I'm thinking of – Good heavens, all those
good people seem to think so much of me—

MR ASLAKSEN: Yes, the people of this town have thought
very highly of you up to now, Doctor.

DR STOCKMANN: Yes, I know, and that's just why I'm
afraid that – Well, what I mean is – when this reaches them
– especially the poorer classes – this summons to take the
town's affairs more into their own hands—

MR HOVSTAD (*rising*): Doctor, I really oughtn't to conceal
from you—

DR STOCKMANN: Aha! I thought there was something up!
But, I tell you, I won't have it! If they're thinking of doing
anything like that—

MR HOVSTAD: Like what?

DR STOCKMANN: Oh, anything – whatever-it-is – a procession, or a dinner, or a subscription-list for a presentation, or anything like that – you must give me your word to put a stop to it! And you too, Mr Aslaksen!

MR HOVSTAD: I'm sorry, Doctor, but before we go any further, we'd better tell you—

Enter MRS KATHERINE STOCKMANN *by entrance door.*

KATHERINE (*sees Dr Stockmann*): Ah – just as I thought!

MR HOVSTAD (*crossing to her*): Why, Mrs Stockmann—?

DR STOCKMANN: Kate! – What on earth are you doing here?

KATHERINE: You know as well as I do.

MR HOVSTAD: Won't you sit down? Or perhaps—

KATHERINE: No, thank you, Mr Hovstad – don't trouble. And you mustn't mind my coming after my husband like this – but I *am* the mother of three children, y'know, and—

DR STOCKMANN: Good gracious, Kate – we all know that.

KATHERINE: Well, you don't seem to be thinking of it very much today – or you wouldn't be so anxious to ruin us all!

DR STOCKMANN: Are you out of your mind, Kate! Just because a man's got a wife and three children, is that to say he isn't to proclaim the truth? – isn't to be a useful citizen? – isn't to do his duty to the town he lives in?

KATHERINE: No, Thomas – but in moderation.

MR ASLAKSEN: That's exactly what I say – everything in moderation.

KATHERINE: And d'you think you're doing right, Mr Hovstad – in enticing my husband away from home and making a fool of him like this?

MR HOVSTAD: I'm not making a fool of anyone—

DR STOCKMANN: Making a fool of me! D'you think I'ld allow anybody to do that!

KATHERINE: Yes, it's just what you would do, Thomas. Oh, I know you've got more brains than the whole town put together, but you're very easily fooled all the same. (*To Mr Hovstad.*) Please, Mr Hovstad, you must understand that, if you print that article he's written, he loses his appointment at the baths—

MR ASLAKSEN: What!

MR HOVSTAD: Well, Doctor, then—

DR STOCKMANN (*laughing*): Ha, ha! – I should like to see them try! No, no, my dear – they'll never go so far as that! Remember, I've got the 'solid majority' behind me!

KATHERINE: Yes, that's just the trouble – if only you had something more sensible and useful behind you!

DR STOCKMANN: Don't be silly, Kate. – Now you run along home and look after the house and leave me to look after the town. How you can be like this when you see me so full of confidence, I don't know! (*Rubs his hands and paces.*) Truth and the people will win, you may be sure of that! Oh, I can see all our enlightened citizens marching together like— (*Stops by chair.*) Why, what on earth's this?

MR ASLAKSEN (*eyeing chair*): Oh, Lord!

MR HOVSTAD (*doing likewise*): Ahem!

DR STOCKMANN: Well, if it isn't the august symbol of authority! (*Takes up the mayor's hat carefully between his finger-tips and exhibits it.*)

KATHERINE: The mayor's hat!

DR STOCKMANN (*waving the stick*): And here's his magic wand, too! . . . But how the devil did they—

MR HOVSTAD: Well, you see—

DR STOCKMANN: Oh, but it's obvious! He's been here trying to talk you over. Ha, ha! – he was counting his chickens too early this time! And the moment he caught sight of me in the printing-office— (*Bursts out laughing.*) he took to his heels! – bolted! – Am I right, Mr Aslaksen?

MR ASLAKSEN (*quickly*): Yes, he took to his heels, Doctor.

DR STOCKMANN: Fled without his stick or his hat – Y'know, that's not like Peter; he never leaves anything behind! Where is he? – What have you done with him? – Ah, of course – in here! Now you'll see, Kate!

KATHERINE: Thomas, please don't – I beg of you—

MR ASLAKSEN: I shouldn't if I were you, Doctor—!

    DR STOCKMANN *places the mayoral hat on his head with a pat, grasps the stick, crosses to door right and throws it open, and springs to a military salute, as enter* PETER STOCKMANN, *purple with rage, and with* MR BILLING *close behind him.*

PETER: And just what's the meaning of all this!

DR STOCKMANN: Show respect now, Peter – Remember, I'm the bigwig in the town now! (*Paces up and down authoritatively.*)

KATHERINE (*almost in tears*): Oh, Thomas!

PETER: Give me that hat and stick!

DR STOCKMANN (*as before*): You may be Chief Constable, but I'm the mayor now! I'm lord of this town!

PETER: Put that hat down, I say! – That's a badge of office and legally bestowed.

DR STOCKMANN: Bah! – D'you imagine that awakening democracy'll go in fear and trembling of a fancy-dress hat? – There'll be a minor revolution in this town tomorrow, you'll see. You thought you could kick me out. – Well, now I shall kick you out, from all your offices and privileged positions! You think I can't, eh? Well, I can! I've got the whole power of society behind me! Hovstad and Billing will thunder in *The Herald* and Aslaksen will attack at the head of the Householders' Association—

MR ASLAKSEN: No, not me, Doctor – I won't . . .

DR STOCKMANN: But of course you will—

PETER: Then perhaps Mr Hovstad intends to take part in this demonstration after all?

MR HOVSTAD: No, your worship, I—

MR ASLAKSEN: No, Mr Hovstad isn't such a fool as to ruin himself and his paper for the sake of an exaggeration . . .

DR STOCKMANN (*looking at him*): What does all this mean, then?

MR HOVSTAD: It appears that you presented your case in a

false light, Doctor – and therefore I'm afraid that I must withdraw my support . . .

MR BILLING: And after what the Mayor was kind enough to tell me in my office, I—

DR STOCKMANN: False light! – Well, that's my responsibility! You just print the article and leave the rest to me; there isn't a word in that article that isn't true and I can prove it!

MR HOVSTAD: I'm sorry, Doctor, I'm not going to print it. I can't . . . I won't . . . I daren't print it!

DR STOCKMANN: You daren't? I never heard such nonsense! – You're the editor – the editor controls the paper, doesn't he?

MR ASLAKSEN: No, Doctor, the subscribers do.

PETER: Fortunately.

MR ASLAKSEN: You see, Doctor, newspapers are controlled by public opinion, by the enlightened mass of the people, by the householders and suchlike . . .

DR STOCKMANN (*calmly*): I see. And they're all against me, is that it?

MR ASLAKSEN: Yes. It'ld mean nothing but ruin for the town if your article were to appear!

DR STOCKMANN: Really? – Is that so—?

PETER: I'll have my hat and stick now, if you don't mind! (DR STOCKMANN *takes off hat and lays it and the stick on table. Picking them up.*) Well, your term of office was short-lived!

DR STOCKMANN: Don't you believe it! (*To Mr Hovstad.*) So you're definitely not going to print my article in *The Herald*?

MR HOVSTAD: No – if only for the sake of your family . . .

KATHERINE: Kindly leave his family out of it, if you don't mind, Mr Hovstad!

PETER (*bringing out envelope from pocket*): The public'll have all the information that's necessary when this appears – it's an official statement. I'll leave it with you, Mr Hovstad.

MR HOVSTAD (*taking it*): Good. Thank you, your worship. I'll see that it appears.

DR STOCKMANN: But not mine – eh? And you think you can silence me and bottle up the truth? Well, you'll find it won't be so easy! Mr Aslaksen – will you please take my article and print it as a pamphlet, at my own expense – I want three, no four, five thousand copies . . .

MR ASLAKSEN: If you offered me its weight in gold, Doctor, I wouldn't use my press for such a purpose. It'ld be flying in the face of public opinion! You won't get it printed anywhere in the town!

DR STOCKMANN: All right – then give it me back.

MR HOVSTAD (*handing it to him*): Here you are, Doctor.

DR STOCKMANN (*taking papers, hat and stick*): It shall reach the public all the same. I shall organize a mass meeting and read it. Everybody in the town'll hear the truth!

PETER: No one in the town'll let you have a hall for such a purpose.

MR ASLAKSEN: No – you won't find anyone, I'm sure.

MR BILLING: Not a soul – and that's a fact!

KATHERINE: Then it's a shame and a disgrace, that's what I say! Why have they all suddenly turned against you like this, Thomas?

DR STOCKMANN (*angrily*): I'll tell you why. – It's because all the men in this town are a lot of old women – like you. All they think about is themselves and their families, they don't care a damn about the rest of the people!

KATHERINE (*taking his arm*): Then I'll show that an old woman can be a man for once! Because from now on I'm going to stand by you, Thomas!

DR STOCKMANN: Thanks, Kate. And don't worry, the truth will come out! If they won't give me a hall, I'll hire a drum and march through the town with it – and I'll read that article at every street corner!

PETER: You wouldn't be such a lunatic as to do a thing like that!

DR STOCKMANN: Oho – wouldn't I?

MR ASLAKSEN: You won't find a single man in the town to march with you!

MR BILLING: No. You won't, y'know – and that's a fact!

KATHERINE: Take no notice of them, Thomas – I'll get the boys to go with you!

DR STOCKMANN: That's a wonderful idea, Kate!

KATHERINE: Morten would love it! – and you know that anything he does Eilif will want to do too!

DR STOCKMANN: Yes, and so will Petra! – And you too, Kate.

KATHERINE: No, I won't – but I'll stand and watch.

DR STOCKMANN (*embracing her*): Bless you, my dear! And now, gentlemen, I'm ready to cross swords with you! And we shall see who wins – you with an 'official statement', or me with the truth! (*Exeunt* DR STOCKMANN *and* KATHERINE *by entrance door.*)

PETER (*shaking his head dubiously*): It looks as though he's turned *her* head, now!

CURTAIN

ACT FOUR

A large old-fashioned room in Captain Horster's house – a couple of evenings later. In the background, open communicating-doors lead to an ante-room, through which is the front door. In the left wall, three high windows, uncurtained. Standing against wall right, approximately centre, a wooden platform and on it a small table, with two candles, a water-bottle, a glass and a little hand-bell. On the wall between the windows are wall-brackets with lighted candles. In the foreground left, a table with candles on it, and by it a chair. Down-right, a door and a few odd chairs.

People of all classes enter by the ante-room until the room is almost full – mostly men, but a few women and a small group of school-boys. They chatter among themselves, exchange greetings, etc.

1ST CITIZEN (*to another nearby*): Hullo, Lamsted – what are you doing here?

2ND CITIZEN: Oh, I never miss a public meeting, if I can help it.

3RD CITIZEN: Brought your whistle with you?

2ND CITIZEN: What d'you think! – You got yours?

3RD CITIZEN: You bet I have! Old Evenson said he was going to bring a cow-horn!

2ND CITIZEN: Good old Evenson!—

Laughter from those nearby.

4TH CITIZEN (*approaching them*): I say, what's it all about? – D'you know what we're here for?

2ND CITIZEN: It's Doctor Stockmann – he's going to have a go at the Mayor!

4TH CITIZEN: The Mayor? – But the Mayor's his brother!

1ST CITIZEN: What's that got to do with it? – The Doctor's not scared of him!

69

3RD CITIZEN: Well, he's in the wrong this time – according to *The Herald*.

2ND CITIZEN: Yes, he must be – because neither the Householders' Association nor the City Club'ld let him have a hall!

1ST CITIZEN: I was told they wouldn't even lend him the one at the baths.

2ND CITIZEN: Well, from what I've heard, I'm not surprised!

1ST MAN (*across the room*): Whose side are we supposed to be on, Henrik – d'you know?

2ND MAN (*next to him*): Keep your eye on Aslaksen and do as he does! – That's what I shall do . . .

Enter MR BILLING *by ante-room, with portfolio under arm, pushing his way through the crowd towards table, left.*

MR BILLING: Excuse me. – Excuse me – thanks. D'you mind if I pass? – I'm reporting for *The Herald*. – Thanks. (*Reaches and sits at table.*)

1ST WORKMAN: Who does he think he is?

2ND WORKMAN: Don't you know him? – That's that Billing chap – he writes for old Aslaksen's paper. . . .

Enter CAPT HORSTER, *with* MRS STOCKMANN *and* PETRA, *and with* EILIF *and* MORTEN *close behind.*

CAPT HORSTER: Now I think you'd better all sit here – then you can easily slip out if things get too lively.

KATHERINE: D'you think there'll be any trouble, then?

CAPT HORSTER: You never know with a crowd like this. Now just sit down and don't worry.

KATHERINE (*sitting*): It was very good of you to give my husband the use of this room.

CAPT HORSTER: Well, as no one else would, I—

PETRA (*sitting*): I think it was a very brave thing to do, Captain Horster.

CAPT HORSTER: Oh, I don't know that there was much bravery about it . . .

Enter HOVSTAD *and* ASLAKSEN *by ante-room, pushing their way through the crowd.*

MR ASLAKSEN (*going up to Capt Horster*): Isn't the Doctor here yet?

CAPT HORSTER: He's waiting in there.

Movement and shuffling in the crowd by ante-room door.

MR HOVSTAD: Look! – Here comes the Mayor!

MR BILLING: Well, I'm damned if he hasn't turned up after all!

Enter PETER STOCKMANN, *making his way through the assembly blandly and bowing politely this way and that, and exchanging a greeting here and there, to take up his position by wall left. A moment later enter* DR STOCKMANN *by door right. He wears a black frock-coat and a white tie. Faint applause, mingled with a little hissing – then silence.*

DR STOCKMANN (*sotto voce*): Are you all right, Kate?

KATHERINE: Quite all right, thank you, Thomas. (*Quietly.*) Now do try and keep your temper, dear.

DR STOCKMANN: Don't worry – I can control myself. (*Looks at his watch, steps on to the platform and bows to the assembly.*) Well, it's a quarter-past, ladies and gentlemen, so I think I'll begin ... (*Takes ms from pocket.*)

MR ASLAKSEN: Oughtn't we to elect a chairman first?

DR STOCKMANN: No, there's no need for that.

SEVERAL MEN: Yes, yes! Let's have a chairman! Aye! A chairman – yes! Yes, yes!

PETER: I certainly think we ought to have a chairman!

DR STOCKMANN: Not for a lecture, Peter – I'm here to deliver a lecture!

PETER: I daresay – but a lecture by the Medical Officer of Health may lead to considerable difference of opinion!

VOICES (*scattered*): Yes, yes! A chairman! (*A whistle or two.*) Let's have a chairman – A chairman!

MR HOVSTAD: It seems that the meeting's in favour of electing a chairman.

DR STOCKMANN (*controlling himself*): Very well, then – let the meeting have its way.

MR ASLAKSEN: Perhaps, the Mayor would be so kind as to do us the honour?

THREE MEN (*applauding vigorously*): Hear, hear! Bravo! Way for the Mayor!

PETER: Thank you, gentlemen. But for reasons which I'm sure you will appreciate, I must ask to be excused. But fortunately we have with us tonight a man who I'm confident will be acceptable to everyone present. I refer of course to the President of the Householders' Association – Mr Aslaksen!

VOICES (*from different parts of the room*): Hear – hear! – Yes! Yes! Bravo Aslaksen! Hooray for Aslaksen!

DR STOCKMANN *takes his ms and descends from the platform with a shrug.*

MR ASLAKSEN: Since it appears to be the unanimous wish of the meeting that I should occupy the chair, I can hardly refuse. . . .

Loud applause and some cheering from the back as MR ASLAKSEN *mounts the platform.*

MR BILLING (*writing*): 'Mr Aslaksen was elected chairman with acclamation . . .'

MR ASLAKSEN: Ladies and gentlemen, since I find myself in the chair, I should just like to say a few brief words. As you know, I am a quiet and peaceable man, who's always held that discreet moderation and – er – and, and moderate discretion, are the best policy. Everyone who knows me knows that!

VOICES (*as before*): Yes, yes! Good old Aslaksen! Hear, hear! Bravo! Hooray! Boo!

MR ASLAKSEN: For I've learnt in the hard school of life and experience that moderation is the one virtue by which a citizen can reveal himself at his best—

PETER: Hear, hear!

MR ASLAKSEN: —And that coupled with discretion best serves the community as a whole! I would therefore urge upon our speaker tonight – who has called this meeting – to strive to keep within the bounds of moderation . . .

A MAN (*by ante-room doorway*): Three cheers for the Temperance Society!

VOICE (*by window*): Go and eat coke! – More beer!

VOICE (*across room*): Hear – hear! – More beer!

VOICES (*scattered*): Sssh! Sssh! Order, order!

MR ASLAKSEN: Now no interruptions, ladies and gentlemen, if you please! Does anyone wish to say anything before we begin?

PETER: Mr Chairman—

MR ASLAKSEN: His worship the Mayor will address the meeting!

PETER: Ladies and gentlemen – in view of my close relationship, of which you're doubtless aware, to the present Medical Officer of Health, I should have preferred not to speak this evening. But my position as Chairman of the Municipal Baths Committee and my natural concern for the vital interests of our town compel me at this stage to move a resolution. I think I'm right in saying that no one here tonight would like to see unreliable and exaggerated accounts of the sanitary condition of both the Baths and of the town itself scattered abroad . . .

VOICES (*scattered*): No, no! Certainly not! Boo! Never! Don't have that! Not likely! No, no!

PETER: Thank you. I therefore move 'that this meeting requires the Medical Officer of the Baths to refrain from publicly delivering his proposed lecture on the subject!'

DR STOCKMANN (*flaring up*): Refrain! – What the blazes—

KATHERINE (*coughing*): Ahem! – H'm!

DR STOCKMANN (*controlling himself*): All right, then. – Well, go on . . .

PETER: In my letter to *The Herald* two days ago, I tried to lay the essential facts before the public – and in such a way that any fair-minded person can easily form his own opinion. I showed that the Medical Officer's proposals – apart from amounting to a vote of censure on the leading men of this town – would saddle the ratepayers with an unwelcome and unnecessary expenditure of at least forty-thousand pounds . . .

Hissing, booing, cat-calls, and sounds of disapproval from nearly the whole assembly.

MR ASLAKSEN (*ringing his bell*): Order ! – Order, please! Ladies and gentlemen, please – Order! I beg to support the Mayor's resolution. I wholeheartedly agree with his worship that there's far more behind this proposal of Doctor Stockmann's than we've been led to believe. Doctor Stockmann talks about the baths, when all the time he's aiming at a revolution! What he really wants is to see our municipal administration in other hands! Now, no one doubts the Doctor's sincerity, nor the honesty of his intentions – there can be no two minds about that. I, myself, am all in favour of self-government by the people – so long as the ratepayers haven't to pay for it! But, in this case, they *would* have to! And that's why I'm damned – I beg your pardon – why I can't possibly support Doctor Stockmann in this particular matter. You can pay too high a price even for gold – at least, that's my opinion!

Loud applause from all sides.

MR HOVSTAD (*rising*): Ladies and gentlemen, I too feel called upon to explain my position. At first Doctor Stockmann's protest certainly appeared to deserve – and to receive – a certain amount of interest, and therefore I supported it as impartially as I could. But before long it appeared that we had been misled by a misrepresentation of the facts—

DR STOCKMANN: Misrepresentation—!

MR HOVSTAD: Well then, by an incomplete view of the facts. . . . This was amply proved by his worship the Mayor's letter! I trust no one here tonight questions my liberal principles – the attitude of *The Herald* on all political matters of importance is well known to every one of you. But in local controversies a local paper must proceed with a certain caution – that I've been taught by men of sound judgment and experience!

MR ASLAKSEN: Hear – hear! – I agree! – I entirely agree!

MR HOVSTAD: And in this matter it has become increasingly clear these last two days that public opinion is against Doctor Stockmann. Now, ladies and gentlemen, what, after all, is the first and foremost duty of an editor? Is it not to work in harmony with his readers? Hasn't he in a way received a tacit mandate to work assiduously and untiringly in the interests of his readers? Or am I mistaken?

VOICES (*scattered*): No, no! He's right! Quite right! Hear, hear! Bravo! (*Whistles.*)

MR HOVSTAD: It's cost me a hard struggle indeed to break with a man in whose house I've been a frequent guest – a man who has up till now, enjoyed the whole-hearted respect and goodwill of his fellow-citizens – a man whose only, or at any rate, whose chief failing is to follow the promptings of his heart rather than of his head!

VOICES (*a few scattered*): Hear – hear! That's true! Good old Doctor! Bravo, Doctor! Hooray!

MR HOVSTAD: But my duty to the public compelled me to take that step. And there is another reason that impels me to oppose him, and, if possible, to restrain him before he goes too far along the road to disaster – consideration for his family . . .

DR STOCKMANN (*rising*): Kindly stick to the water-supply and the drains!

MR HOVSTAD: —Consideration, I say, for his wife and his unprovided children!

MORTEN (*sotto voce*): Does he mean us, Mother?

KATHERINE: Sssh, dear!

MR ASLAKSEN: I will now put his worship the Mayor's resolution to the vote! . . .

DR STOCKMANN: There's no need! – I've no intention of saying anything tonight about the filth at the baths! No – I've something quite different to say!

PETER (*as though to himself*): What's coming now, I wonder?

A DRUNK (*from ante-room doorway*): I'm a ratepayer, so I've got an opinion! And you say I'm right! My firm, shakable and unutterable opinion is—

VOICE: Be quiet at the back there! He's drunk!

VOICES (*scattered*): Shut up! – Order! Throw him out! Send him home to his missus! Shame! He's drunk! Turn him out! Disgraceful! Out with him! Chuck him out!

A scuffle with loud and incoherent protests from the Drunk in the ante-room – then quiet.

DR STOCKMANN: Please! May I be allowed to speak?

MR ASLAKSEN (*rising and ringing his bell*): Quiet! Order! Ladies and gentlemen! Order, please! Doctor Stockmann will now address the meeting!

DR STOCKMANN: Thank you. Ladies and gentlemen, I should like to have seen anyone dare to try muzzling me a few days ago, as has been done here tonight! I'd have fought tooth and nail for my rights! But tonight it doesn't matter, because I've other and far more important things to speak about!

The CROWD press closer, settle down with a little coughing. MORTEN KIIL pushes himself into sight.

DR STOCKMANN (*continuing*): I've pondered a great deal the last couple of days, pondered over so many things, considered so many problems, that at last they made my head spin . . .

PETER (*coughing*): Ahem!

DR STOCKMANN: However, eventually it cleared and I was able to see things in their true perspective! And that's why I'm standing here tonight! Because ladies and gentlemen,

I've a revelation to make! – I've made a discovery! Oh, something of far greater moment than the mere fact that our water-supply is polluted and that the ground on which our health-resort stands is riddled with pestilence!

VOICES (*scattered; shouting*): Not the baths! Keep the baths out of it! Boo! Don't mention the baths! Shame! (*Hisses.*) Shut up! (*Cat-calls.*) We won't listen!

DR STOCKMANN: I said a discovery! The discovery that our whole moral life is polluted, and that our whole social existence is itself rooted in the pestilent soil of falsehood!

VOICES (*scattered and murmuring in astonishment*): What's that? Moral life? Fancy! What's he say? Well, I never! What's he getting at?

PETER: Such an insinuation—!

MR ASLAKSEN (*with hand on bell*): I must ask the speaker to moderate his language!

DR STOCKMANN: Now I've loved my native town as only a man *can* love the place where he spent his childhood! I was still a young man when I left it – and distance, absence, and memories soon cast a warm glow for me over both the town and its people . . . (*Scattered cries of approval – and some applause.*) Then, for years, I was buried in that hole up north. My patients were thinly scattered over a bleak and stony wilderness – and poor, undernourished creatures they were, too. I often had the uneasy feeling that they'd have been far better off with a vet than with a doctor!

A murmur runs through the assembly.

MR BILLING (*laying down his pen*): Well, I'm damned if I ever heard—!

MR HOVSTAD: It's a downright insult to decent country-folk!

DR STOCKMANN: Please! – Just a moment! – I don't think anyone here can accuse me of having forgotten you all while I was away! I was like an eider-duck, brooding on her nest – only what I hatched out was the plan for the Baths! (*Applause and faint protests.*) And when, at last, fate happily decreed that

I was to come home again, then, ladies and gentlemen, it
seemed to me that I hadn't another wish in the world. Or,
rather, I had just one: a sincere and ardent longing to be of
some service to my native town and the people who lived
there.

PETER (*staring ahead*): Well, you certainly choose a peculiar
way of doing it – ahem!

DR STOCKMANN: But, y'know, I was seeing everything
through the half-closed eyes of the day-dreamer! But
yesterday morning – well, yesterday afternoon, to be exact –
my eyes were opened in no uncertain manner; and the first
thing I saw was the colossal stupidity of the municipal
authorities—

  Shouting, hubbub and laughter. MRS STOCKMANN *coughs
  significantly.*

PETER: Mr Chairman!

MR ASLAKSEN (*ringing his bell*): Doctor – as Chairman I
must—!

DR STOCKMANN: Don't be so petty as to take me up on a
word, Mr Aslaksen! All I mean is that I suddenly realized
what a sorry mess our leading men had made of things down
at the Baths! And, if there's one thing I can't stand, it's
'leading men'! – I've seen too many of 'em in my time!
They're like goats in a garden! They damage everything they
touch. They stand in your way wherever you turn. – I should
like to see the whole damn lot of them exterminated like any
other vermin—!

  General uproar and protest.

PETER: Mr Chairman, are such expressions to be allowed?

MR ASLAKSEN (*with hand on bell*): Dr Stock—?

DR STOCKMANN: The only thing that really bothers me is
why it took me so long to tumble to it! – Especially, when
I had such a superb example right under my very nose
almost every day of the week – my own brother Peter – slow-
witted – enormously prejudiced—

Laughter, hubbub, whistles, cat-calls and hisses. MRS STOCK-
MANN *coughs warningly.* MR ASLAKSEN *rings his bell
furiously.* THE DRUNK *has found his way in again.*

DRUNK: If he means me – the name's Petersen, with a sen . . .
I'll knock his – if he's talking about me – I will! I'm not
afraid of – Hey! What the—!

VOICES (*scattered*): Throw him out! It's that drunk! Quiet!
Chuck him out! Order! Shame! Out with him! Disgraceful!

A scuffle in the doorway of the ante-room – then quiet again.

PETER: Who is that man?

1ST CITIZEN: I don't know, Mr Mayor – I've never seen
him before. . . .

2ND CITIZEN: He doesn't live in the town.

3RD CITIZEN: I think he's a boilermaker from down—

MR ASLAKSEN: He was obviously drunk. Carry on, Doctor –
but, please, with a little more moderation . . .

DR STOCKMANN: Very well, gentlemen, I shall say no more
about our leading townsmen! And if anyone imagines from
what I've just said that I'm out to make a clean sweep of them
all, he's wrong – quite wrong! Because I'm pretty sure that
these comfortable time-servers, these ageing relics of a dying
system, are industriously digging their own graves – and
they don't need a push from a doctor! But it isn't men like
that who are the real danger to the town. It isn't they who
are chiefly responsible for poisoning our moral environment,
and infecting the ground we walk on. It isn't they who are
the most dangerous enemies of truth, freedom and progress
among us—!

VOICES (*scattered*): Who is, then? Who is? Who? – Give us
their names! Tell us who it is! Name them! Names! Name
them!

DR STOCKMANN: Don't worry – I'm going to! Because
that's precisely the discovery I made yesterday! (*Raising his
voice.*) The greatest menace to truth and progress among us
is what we call the 'solid majority'! Yes – the damned, solid,

liberal majority! That, and that alone, is what stands in our light! – And now you know!

Terrific uproar, with almost everyone shouting, whistling, hissing, booing and cat-calling. Several of the older men exchange surreptitious glances of satisfaction. MRS STOCKMANN *rises anxiously, while* EILIF *and* MORTEN *advance threateningly towards several of the schoolboys who are making unseemly noises.* MR ASLAKSEN *rings his bell violently and calls desperately for order.* MESSRS HOVSTAD *and* BILLING *both speak but their words are drowned. Eventually, order is restored.*

MR ASLAKSEN: Order! Quiet! Ladies and gentlemen – Order – Order, please! – Thank you! . . . I must call upon the speaker to withdraw his ill-considered expressions!

DR STOCKMANN: Never – never, Mr Aslaksen! It's the majority in this town that denies me my freedom and tries to prevent my speaking the truth!

MR HOVSTAD: The majority always has right on its side!

MR BILLING: And truth as well! That's a fact!

DR STOCKMANN: That's just where you're wrong! The majority *never* has right on its side – never, I say! That's just one of those social fallacies which any fair-minded individualist has to fight against! After all, who constitutes the majority in any country? The wise men or the fools? And it's the same all the world over – the fools are in an absolute and overwhelming majority – and you can't deny it! But for heaven's sake don't suggest that it's right and proper for the fools to govern the wise! (*Cries, boos and general uproar.*) Oh yes, you can shout me down – but you can't prove me wrong! The majority has might, unfortunately – but it hasn't right! It's I, and a few like me, who are right! The minority's always right! (*Renewed uproar.*)

MR HOVSTAD: Ah – so you've become an aristocrat since the day before yesterday, eh, Doctor?

DR STOCKMANN: I've already said that I'm not going to

waste another word on that feeble, narrow-chested, short-winded crew we're rapidly leaving behind us! – The thrill of life has left them! I'm talking about the all too few individuals among us who've seen and accepted new and vital truths! – pioneers of progress! – that stand, as it were, at the outposts, so far ahead that the 'solid majority' hasn't yet been able to catch up with them! – And there they are, fighting for truths that are too newly born into the world of truth to have more than a handful of supporters!

MR HOVSTAD: So the doctor's a revolutionary now!

DR STOCKMANN: For once you're right, Mr Hovstad! I am! I'm in revolt against the lie that truth is always vested in the majority! For what sort of truths does the majority favour? – Truths that are so old that they're giving at the joints! And when a truth's as old as that, ladies and gentlemen, it's well on the way to becoming a lie! (*Laughter and cat-calls.*) Yes – though you may not believe it – truths are by no means the hardy Methuselahs some people imagine! The life of normally constituted truths is about seventeen or eighteen years – seldom more than twenty. And the scraggier they get, the less nourishing they are! Yet it's only then that the majority considers them fit for human consumption, and recommends them as good wholesome food! As a doctor, I can assure you there's little nourishment in that sort of fare! 'Majority truths' are like last year's salt pork or mouldy ham – the cause of all the moral scurvy that ravages Society!

MR ASLAKSEN: I respectfully suggest that the speaker is wandering from the subject!

PETER: I agree with you, Mr Chairman.

DR STOCKMANN: That's an absurd thing to say, Peter. – I'm keeping to the subject as closely as I possibly can! – And the subject's precisely this: that it's the masses, the majority, this damned 'solid majority' – that's poisoning the sources of our moral vitality and infecting the ground we walk on!

MR HOVSTAD: And you're saying all this just because the

vast majority of discriminating people is sensible enough to accept only well-tried and acknowledged truths?

DR STOCKMANN: Rubbish, my dear Mr Hovstad! Well-tried truths, he says! That's just the trouble! Don't you realize that the truths acknowledged by the masses today are simply those proclaimed by the pioneers in our grandfathers' time? We pioneers of today don't acknowledge them any longer! In fact, I believe there's only one indisputable truth – and that is that no society can ever thrive on such old and fossilized truths!

MR HOVSTAD: Instead of all this abstract talk, it might be more interesting if you gave us some examples of these fossilized truths we're supposed to be living on?

Applause from several quarters.

DR STOCKMANN: I could give you a whole string of 'em! For the moment, I'm going to confine myself to one – one acknowledged truth, which is actually one of the most outrageous lies ever propounded, but on which Mr Hovstad *and The Herald and* it's readers are constantly nourished!

MR HOVSTAD: Really? – And what's that?

DR STOCKMANN: The doctrine you've inherited from your ancestors and still persist in spreading far and wide – the doctrine that the public, the masses, the multitude is the essence of the people; that the common man – the untrained, inexperienced man-in-the-street has the same right to approve and to condemn, to counsel and to govern, as the qualified intellectually few!

MR BILLING: Well, I'm damned if I—!

MR HOVSTAD (*shouting simultaneously*): Remember that, my fellow-citizens! Make a note of that!

VOICES (*scattered – angrily*): We aren't the people – aren't we! Not fit to govern, eh? – Only the rich can rule!

A WORKMAN: Chuck him out for talking like that! Chuck him out!

ANOTHER: Yes, out with him!

2ND CITIZEN (*calling*): Blow your horn, Evenson!

   Loud blasts of a cow-horn, accompanied by whistles, boos, hisses, cat-calls and general uproar.

DR STOCKMANN (*when the noise has subsided a little*): Be reasonable! For Heaven's sake, be reasonable! Can't you bear to hear the truth just for once? I don't expect you all to agree with me – not just yet, anyhow. But I must say I expected Mr Hovstad to be on my side, once he recovered himself! – After all, Mr Hovstad claims to be a freethinker—!

VOICES (*several scattered, murmuring in astonishment*): Freethinker? – Hovstad? Well! Hovstad a freethinker, did he say? Not Hovstad, surely! Hovstad is? Well, I'm—! Funny that!

MR HOVSTAD (*shouting*): Prove it, Doctor Stockmann! Go on – just prove it! When have I ever said so in print? Tell me that!

DR STOCKMANN (*reflecting*): No, damnit, that's true! – You've never had the courage! Well, I won't make it awkward for you, Mr Hovstad. Let's say I'm the freethinker, then. And now I'm going to prove to you all, scientifically, that *The Herald* is leading you by the nose when it tells you that the masses are the backbone of the nation. It's just another newspaper lie, I tell you! The masses are simply the raw material from which a people is fashioned! (*Hubbub, jeers, laughter.*) Well, isn't it like that with any living creature you care to name? Isn't there a world of difference between pedigree and ordinary animals? Take a common barn-door hen – is it worth eating? It's practically all skin and bone! – And what are the eggs like? – Why, a good healthy crow or raven can lay very nearly as good! Put beside it a pedigree Spanish or Japanese hen, or a good pheasant or turkey – you'll soon see the difference! Take the dog – man's best friend. Think of an ordinary mongrel, ragged, coarse-haired, misshappen, running about the streets and using doorways instead of lamp-posts; compare him with a pedigree poodle, brought up in a fine house, on good food, used to the sound of soft voices and music. Don't you think its brain is very differently developed from that of the mongrel? Of course it is! You've seen them yourselves at circuses performing all sorts of tricks, a mongrel could never do – even if he tried from now till kingdom come!

General uproar and cat-calls.

1ST CITIZEN (*calling*): You're telling us we're dogs then?

3RD CITIZEN: We're not animals, y'know, Doctor!

DR STOCKMANN: Ah – but that's just what we are, my friend! – whether we like it or not! – The very highest type of animal no doubt; but even among us there are all too few of the finest breed! There's a world of difference between poodle-type and the mongrel-type man! And the funny part of it is – Mr Hovstad here entirely agrees with me so long as I keep to four-footed animals! Don't you, Mr Hovstad?

MR HOVSTAD: Oh yes, it's true enough where animals are concerned!

DR STOCKMANN: There you are, you see! But the moment I apply the argument to the two-legged variety, Mr Hovstad stops short! He hasn't the courage to carry his convictions to their logical conclusion. So he turns the whole thing upside down, and tells you in *The Herald* that it's the barn-door hen and the street mongrel that are the finest specimens in our menagerie. But that's always the way when we cannot shed our common mental heritage and achieve intellectual superiority!

MR HOVSTAD: I lay no claim to any sort of superiority! I come of honest, hardworking country-folk; and I'm proud that my origin should be rooted deep down among the people you're choosing to insult!

VOICES (*mostly working-class – calling*): Hooray! Good old Hovstad! Bravo, Hovstad! Bravo! Hear – hear! Go on! – Tell him some more! Hooray!

DR STOCKMANN: But the kind of common people I'm alluding to aren't to be found only among the rank and file, y'know! They crawl and swarm all round us! Why, you've only got to look at his worship – your own smug and gentlemanly mayor! – My brother's as clearly one of the common people as any man that walks on two legs!

General laughter and hisses.

PETER: I protest! – I protest against these personal allusions! Mr Chairman—

DR STOCKMANN (*imperturbably*): —and that not because he, like myself, is descended from some old cut-throat of a pirate from Pomerania or thereabouts – for that's what we are—

PETER: A ridiculous story! It's quite untrue!

DR STOCKMANN: —but simply because he takes his thoughts from those above him and holds the same opinions as they do! Those who do that belong, intellectually speaking, to the masses. – And that's why my superior brother's so inferior, and hasn't a liberal thought in his head!

PETER: Mr Chairman, I—!

MR HOVSTAD: So it's only the superior people in this country who are liberal? – Well, that's something new, if you like!

General laughter and hubbub.

DR STOCKMANN: Yes – I told you I'd made a discovery! And here's another part of it – that liberal thinking is almost exactly the same as morality! Therefore I say it's unpardonable of *The Herald* to go on proclaiming day after day the false doctrine that it's the masses, the multitude, the 'solid majority' who are the keepers of liberal doctrine and morality! – and that vice, corruption and depravity flow from culture, just as all the muck flows down from the tanneries up at Molledal into our Baths water! (*General uproar, cat-calls, hisses, boos, etc. Going on imperturbably, smiling with enthusiasm.*) Yet this same *Herald* keeps crying out for a higher standard of living for the masses! Why, if *The Herald* is to be relied upon, elevating the masses like that would simply be consigning them to perdition! Fortunately, the idea that culture is demoralizing is just another fabrication that's been handed down to us! No; it's ignorance, poverty and dirt that do the devil's work! In a home that isn't properly aired and swept every day – my wife says floors ought to be well-scrubbed too, but that's asking a bit too much. – Well, in a house like that, within two or three years the occupants lose the power to think or act morally. Lack of oxygen weakens the conscience. And I must say there seems to be precious little oxygen in many of the houses here, since the entire 'solid majority' is unscrupulous enough to want the future prosperity of the town to be built on a quagmire of lies and deceit!

MR ASLAKSEN: I can't allow such a serious accusation to be levelled against a whole community!

1ST CITIZEN: I move that the chairman direct the speaker to sit down.

VOICES (*scattered and angry*): Hear – hear! Sit down! Quite right! It's an insult! Yes, sit down! Shut up! Shame! Sit down, Stockmann! Chuck him out! Hear – hear!

DR STOCKMANN (*flaring up*): Right! – then I'll shout the truth at every street corner! I'll write to the papers in other towns! I'll let the whole country know what's going on here!

MR HOVSTAD (*rising*): In fact, your one idea's to ruin the town, eh, Doctor?

DR STOCKMANN: Yes. I've so much regard for it, I'ld rather see it ruined than prospering on a lie!

MR ASLAKSEN: This is getting beyond a joke!

 General uproar – hisses, cat-calls, etc. MRS STOCKMANN *coughs, but to no avail.*

MR HOVSTAD (*shouting above the din*): A man who'd say a thing like that is nothing but an enemy of the people!

DR STOCKMANN (*with mounting fervour*): What does it matter

if a community that lives on deceit *is* ruined? I say it ought to be razed to the ground! All men who live by lies should be exterminated – like vermin! At this rate you'll contaminate the whole country – with the result that the whole country'll deserve to be ruined! And, if that ever happens, I shall say from the bottom of my heart – 'Let the country fall! Let the people perish!'

VOICES (*from various quarters*): Hovstad's right – he's an enemy of the people! Shame! He's an enemy all right! It's disgraceful! An enemy of the people, that's what he is! Shame!

MR BILLING (*excitedly*): D'you hear that, Doctor? – Listen to 'em! – The voice of the people!

VOICES (*almost the entire assembly*): He's an enemy! He hates us, that's what he does! Hates his own country! Shame! Boo! Enemy of the people! Chuck him out! Enemy of the people!

MR ASLAKSEN (*ringing bell*): Both as a citizen of this town and as a private individual I'm shocked by what we've had to listen to tonight! Doctor Stockmann has revealed himself in a light I should never have thought possible. Nevertheless, I feel I must subscribe to the opinion of so many of my fellow-citizens; and I think we ought to express it in a formal resolution. I therefore beg to move that 'This meeting declares Doctor Thomas Stockmann, the Medical Officer of Health, to be an enemy of the people!'

Wild applause, cheering, shouting and cat-calling. Several nearest gather round Dr Stockmann and hiss him. MRS STOCKMANN *and* PETRA *rise apprehensively, while* EILIF *and* MORTEN *go into battle with their former assailants, but are quickly separated by some of their elders.*

DR STOCKMANN (*to those hooting him*): Fools! You're just near-sighted fools, that's all! – Fools! I tell you, you're nothing but a lot of—

MR ASLAKSEN (*ringing bell*): You're out of order in speaking now, Doctor – a formal vote on the motion must now be taken. But, out of consideration for personal feelings it shall be taken by ballot. Have you got any paper there, Mr Billing?

MR BILLING: Yes, Mr Chairman – white and blue—

MR ASLAKSEN (*crossing to him*): Good – that'll be the quickest way. Tear it into strips – yes, like that, that's right. (*To the assembly.*) Now please! Silence! Order please! A blue slip means 'no' – a white one 'yes'. I shall come round and collect the votes myself!

Exit PETER STOCKMANN *pushing his way through the crowd, while* MR ASLAKSEN *and a couple of others go round with hats containing the slips.*

1ST CITIZEN (*to Mr Hovstad*): What on earth's the matter with Stockmann? – D'you know what sent him off like that?

MR HOVSTAD: Oh, you know what a madcap he is!

2ND CITIZEN (*to Mr Billing*): You spend a lot of time at the house – have you never noticed if the fellow drinks?

MR BILLING: I'm damned if I know, really. There's never any shortage – always plenty going, so to speak . . .

3RD CITIZEN: No – he gets – what d'you call 'em? – *brain-storms*, that's his trouble!

1ST CITIZEN: I wonder if there's insanity in the family?

MR BILLING: Now that wouldn't surprise me in the least!

4TH CITIZEN: No – it's just sheer malice; he wants to get his own back for something or other.

MR BILLING: I know he was after a rise in salary not so long ago; but he didn't get it!

CITIZENS (*together*): Ah, that's it, then. That accounts for it! Of course! That explains everything!

DRUNK (*who has got in again*): Gimme a blue one, that's what I want! Well, c'mon, give it me –Why don't you give me a white one? That's it, that's the one, that's not blue! Now I want a white one, too – and then I've got a blue one! *I'll* show what a—

VOICES (*scattered*): It's that drunk again! Chuck him out! Out with him! It's disgraceful! Oughtn't to be allowed!

MORTEN KIIL (*going up to Dr Stockmann*): Well, Stockmann, now you can see how these crazy ideas of yours go down!

DR STOCKMANN: I've done my duty.

MORTEN KIIL: What was that you said about the tanneries up at Molledal?

DR STOCKMANN: You heard all right – that's where all the muck comes from!

MORTEN KIIL: From mine as well?

DR STOCKMANN: Yours, unfortunately, is the worst of the lot.

MORTEN KIIL: And are you going to put that in the papers, too?

DR STOCKMANN: I can't hide anything.

MORTEN KIIL: Very well – but I warn you, Stockmann, you may pay dearly for it if you do! (*Exit, pushing his way through crowd.*)

FAT MAN (*approaching Capt Horster, and ignoring the ladies*): Well, Captain Horster, so you lend your house to enemies of the people?

CAPT HORSTER: Presumably, I can do as I like with my own property, Mr Vik.

FAT MAN: Then you can have no objection if I do the same with mine!

CAPT HORSTER: What d'you mean, sir?

FAT MAN: You shall hear from me in the morning. (*Turns and exit, pushing his way through crowd.*)

PETRA: Wasn't that the owner of your ship, Captain Horster?

CAPT HORSTER: Yes, that was Mr Vik.

MR ASLAKSEN (*mounting the platform, clutching ballot slips and ringing bell*): Order! Order, please, gentlemen! Order! Now! . . . I wish to announce the result! By all the votes except one—

A YOUNG MAN: That's the drunk, I expect!

MR ASLAKSEN: —from an intoxicated intruder – this meeting declares Doctor Thomas Stockmann to be an enemy of the people! (*Shouts and applause.*) Three cheers for our grand old town! – Hip, hip—

THE CROWD: Hooray! – etc.

MR ASLAKSEN: Three cheers for that able and hardworking citizen, who has so loyally set aside all family feelings – his worship the mayor! Hip, hip—

THE CROWD: Hooray! – etc.

MR ASLAKSEN: The meeting is dissolved! (*Descends from platform.*)

MR BILLING: Three cheers for our honourable chairman – Mr Aslaksen! – Hip, hip—

THE CROWD: Hooray! – etc.

DR STOCKMANN: My hat and coat, Petra. Captain Horster – can you find room for passengers to the United States?

CAPT HORSTER: For you and your family, Doctor – we'll make room somehow.

DR STOCKMANN (*as* PETRA *helps him on with his coat*): Good. Come on, Kate – come along, boys! (*Gives her his arm.*)

KATHERINE (*sotto voce*): Thomas dear, let's get out by the back way.

DR STOCKMANN: No back ways for me, Kate. (*Raises his voice.*) You'll hear more from this enemy of the people, before he shakes the dust from his feet! I'm not so forgiving as a certain Person – I shan't say – 'Forgive you, for you know not what you do!'

MR ASLAKSEN (*shouting*): That's blasphemy, Doctor Stockmann – sheer blasphemy!

MR BILLING: Dammit, I've never heard anything like it!

VOICE (*coarse, in doorway*): Threatening us now, is he?

VOICES (*from several quarters, excitedly*): Let's go and smash his windows! Duck him! Yes, yes! Duck him! Hooray! Duck him in the fjord!

VOICE (*from another part of the room*): Come on, Evenson –
blow your horn, man – blow it!

Horn-blowing, whistling, cat-calls and shouting, as DR
STOCKMANN *and his family push their way through the crowd
to the front door –* CAPT HORSTER *clearing a path for them –
exeunt.*

OMNES (*shouting after them*): Enemy of the people! After
them! Duck him! Enemy of the people! Enemy of the
people!

MR BILLING (*putting his things into his portfolio*): Well! *I'm* not
drinking toddy at the Stockmanns' tonight – and *that's* a
fact!

The CROWD *push and shove towards the ante-room and front
door, and the uproar continues – the shouting has been taken up by
others outside, and gradually gives way to a chant – 'Enemy of the
People!' – 'Enemy of the People!' – etc.*

CURTAIN

ACT FIVE

Dr Stockmann's consulting-room – the following morning. Book-
shelves and glass cases filled with specimens, bottles, etc., line the
walls. Left-back, a door leads to the hall; down-left, another to the
sitting-room. In wall right, two windows, of which most of the
panes are broken. Left, against the wall, a flat, backless couch.
Centre, a writing-table, littered with books, journals, etc. – and by
it a chair. Right, an arm-chair and by it an occasional table.

DR STOCKMANN *in dressing-gown, slippers and a smoking-cap, is*
bending down and raking about under one of the wall-cases with
an umbrella. After a few moments, he meets with success and edges
out a couple of small stones.

DR STOCKMANN (*calling into sitting-room*): I've just found
another couple, Kate!

KATHERINE (*off-stage from sitting-room, calling*): Oh, you'll
find plenty more yet, I expect.

DR STOCKMANN (*adding the stones to a small heap on the writing-*
table): I'll keep these as souvenirs – they'll serve as reminders
for Eilif and Morten, and they can have them when they
grow up. (*Rakes about under bookcase – calls.*) Hasn't – oh,
what the devil's the girl's name? – Hasn't she been for the
glazier yet?

Enter MRS STOCKMANN *by sitting-room door.*

KATHERINE: Yes, but he said he wasn't sure if he could get
round today.

DR STOCKMANN: He's afraid to – that's what he means.

KATHERINE: Yes, Randina thought that too – on account of
the neighbours. (*Calling off-stage into sitting-room.*) Yes, what
is it, Randina? – Oh, all right – I'll come and get it . . . (*Exit*

into sitting-room, and returns a moment later.) Here's a letter for you, Thomas.

DR STOCKMANN: Well, give it to me . . . (*Straightens up – takes letter, opens it and reads.*) Aha—!

KATHERINE: Who's it from?

DR STOCKMANN: Our dear landlord! – Notice to quit.

KATHERINE: Oh no! – I can't believe it. – And he's such a nice man, too . . .

DR STOCKMANN (*scanning letter*): Well, there it is! – He daren't do otherwise, he says. – It's against his principles to do it, but in the circumstances, can't help himself – on account of his fellow-citizens – out of respect for public opinion – isn't a free agent – daren't offend certain influential persons . . .

KATHERINE: There, you see, Thomas!

DR STOCKMANN: Yes, yes, I see all right! They're all alike in this town – every one of 'em! Not a single one of 'em dares do anything for fear of the others! (*Throws down letter disgustedly on writing-table.*) Anyhow, it doesn't matter to us now, Kate – we shall soon be on the high seas, and then—

KATHERINE: But are you quite sure we're doing the right thing, Thomas?

DR STOCKMANN: Surely you don't expect me to remain here? – What, when I've been branded – pilloried as an enemy of the people – had my windows smashed? Yes, and not only that – look, Kate – they've torn a great hole in my new trousers!

KATHERINE: Oh dear yes, so they have – and they're your Sunday ones!

DR STOCKMANN: There's a moral in that, Kate! – A man should never wear his best trousers when he goes out to fight for truth and freedom! Anyhow, it isn't the trousers – you can always work wonders for me with a needle and thread! It's just that the mob, the rabble, should dare to attack me like that, as if they were my equals – that's what riles me!

KATHERINE: Yes, I know, Thomas – I know they've behaved very badly to you, dear – but is that really sufficient reason for leaving the country?

DR STOCKMANN: My dear Kate, don't you think they're just as bad in other towns? Take my word for it, dear, they're all alike! Well, let the dogs bark, that's not what really matters; it's the fact that every single person in this country is the slave of his party! Not that I imagine it's so very different over there. I expect the country's rampant with 'solid majorities', liberal movements, and all the rest of the blasted humbug. But at least they don't do things by halves – they may kill you, but they won't slowly torture you to death! They don't screw a free man's soul in a vice as they do here! And the country's big; if necessary you can get away from it all! (*Paces.*) If only I knew where there was a virgin forest, or a small South Sea island for sale cheap—

KATHERINE: Yes, but think of the boys, Thomas!

DR STOCKMANN: You are a funny woman, Kate! D'you mean to say you'ld rather have the boys grow up in a society like this? Why, you saw for yourself last night that half the population's out of its wits and, if the other half isn't, that's only because it hasn't got any wits to lose!

KATHERINE: Thomas dear, you mustn't mind my saying this, but I do think that some of the things you called them may have had a little to do with it, y'know . . .

DR STOCKMANN: But wasn't it the truth I told them? – Every word of it? *Don't* they turn every idea upside down? *Don't* they get even right and wrong into a most unholy tangle? Don't they say that things I know are true, are nothing but lies? And the most ridiculous part of it is that all these so-called Liberals are adult men, going about persuading themselves and everyone else that they stand for freedom and progress! I ask you, Kate, did you ever hear anything like it?

KATHERINE: Yes, I suppose you're right, dear, but— (*Enter*

PETRA *from sitting-room*.) Why, Petra – you're back early!

PETRA: Yes, I know – I've just been dismissed.

KATHERINE: Dismissed!

DR STOCKMANN: You too, eh?

PETRA: Mrs Busk sent for me this morning and told me I was to leave at the end of term, so I thought it best to leave at once—

DR STOCKMANN: Quite right!

KATHERINE: Well, I must say I'm surprised at Mrs Busk's doing a thing like that – she always struck me as such a nice woman.

PETRA: Oh Mother, it isn't Mrs Busk. She hated doing it, I could see that. But she said she daren't do otherwise – so here I am!

DR STOCKMANN (*laughing and rubbing his hands*): Daren't! – so she's another of 'em. Oh, it's magnificent!

KATHERINE: Well, after that dreadful scene last night—

PETRA: Oh, it wasn't only that . . .

DR STOCKMANN: Well?

PETRA: Mrs Busk showed me no less than three letters she'd received this morning.

DR STOCKMANN: And I bet they were anonymous!

PETRA: Yes, as a matter of fact, they were.

DR STOCKMANN: You see – they daren't even sign their names, Kate!

PETRA: Two of them say that a certain man, who's been a frequent guest here, said at the club last night that I hold extremely emancipated views on various subjects—

DR STOCKMANN: You didn't deny it, I hope?

PETRA: Most certainly not – I should not dream of it! Mrs Busk's own views are fairly emancipated, anyhow – at least they are when we're alone together. But now it's come out – and I suppose everyone's talking about it – she simply daren't keep me on.

KATHERINE: Someone who's been our guest, too! There,

you see, Thomas, that shows you the return you get for your hospitality.

DR STOCKMANN: We're not going on living in this plague-spot any longer! Pack up everything, Kate, as quick as you can. – The sooner we can get away the better!

KATHERINE: Sssh! – I think there's someone in the hall. See who it is, Petra, there's a dear . . .

PETRA (*crossing and opening hall door*): Oh, it's you, Captain Horster – do come in . . .

Enter CAPT HORSTER *by hall door*.

CAPT HORSTER: Good morning. I thought I'd just look in and see how you are . . .

DR STOCKMANN (*shaking hands with him*): Thanks – that's very nice of you . . .

KATHERINE: And thank you for helping us home like that last night, Captain Horster.

PETRA: But how did you ever manage to get home yourself?

CAPT HORSTER: Oh, I managed. I can be quite a tough customer y'know – and those chaps bark far worse than they bite!

DR STOCKMANN: Yes, it's astonishing what cowards they are, when it comes to it! Look – I'll show you something! These are all the stones they threw through the windows! Just look at them! Have you ever seen such a miserable pile? There aren't more than two decent-sized ones in the whole lot! The rest are just pebbles – gravel! And d'you know, they stood out there shouting and swearing that they'd break every bone in my body? But as for *doing* anything? – Oh, no! I tell you, Horster, that's something you'll never see in *this* town!

CAPT HORSTER: And lucky for you this time, Doctor!

DR STOCKMANN: Yes, I suppose so. But it's a sad thought all the same. I shudder to think what would happen if ever it came to a real national crisis – why, public opinion would vote for taking to one's heels, and the 'solid majority' would turn tail like a flock of sheep, Captain Horster. That's what I find so depressing – and, y'know, it really worries me. But, dammit – what's it got to do with me, anyhow! – They've called me an enemy of the people! – Well then, I'll be one!

KATHERINE: You'll never be that, dear – and you know it!

DR STOCKMANN: Don't be too sure, Kate. A nasty name on one's innocence can be like a spot on the lung, you know. And *such* a name! – I can't get it out of my mind. It nags at me all the time – like acid in the tummy . . . Only it's no good taking soda bicarb for *that*!

PETRA: Oh, you should just laugh at them, Father!

CAPT HORSTER: They'll think differently one day, Doctor.

KATHERINE: Yes, that's true, dear, as sure as we're all standing here!

DR STOCKMANN: Yes – perhaps – when it's too late – and they've only themselves to thank for it! Then they can just go on wallowing in their own dirt and curse the day they drove a true patriot into exile . . . By the way, when d'you sail, Captain Horster?

CAPT HORSTER: Well – that's really what I came to tell you about—

DR STOCKMANN: Nothing wrong with the ship, I hope?

CAPT HORSTER: No – she's sound enough; but it looks as if I shan't be sailing in her this time.

PETRA: You don't mean to say you've been dismissed?

CAPT HORSTER (*smiling*): Yes – I'm going to be a land-lubber for a bit.

PETRA: You too!

KATHERINE: There, you see, Thomas!

DR STOCKMANN: Just because you stand up for the truth! If I'ld have dreamt that anything like this could—

CAPT HORSTER: Oh, don't let it worry you. I shall soon get another ship – there are plenty of other companies.

DR STOCKMANN: I'm certainly surprised at Vik! I should

have thought that a rich man like that, independent . . . It's downright disgraceful!

CAPT HORSTER: Oh, he's not a bad sort in his way . . . He said he'ld like to keep me on, if he dared—

DR STOCKMANN: But he didn't dare? No, of course not!

CAPT HORSTER: He said it wasn't so easy for him, being a party-man—

DR STOCKMANN: Ah – there he hit the nail on the head! A party's like a sausage machine – it minces all the brains up together and turns them out as fat-heads and block-heads!

KATHERINE: Now Thomas dear—!

PETRA (*to Capt Horster*): If you hadn't seen us home, perhaps this would never have happened . . .

CAPT HORSTER: Oh, I don't regret it.

PETRA (*giving him her hand*): Thank you for that, Captain Horster.

CAPT HORSTER (*to Dr Stockmann*): Anyhow, what I came to say was this – if you're really determined to go away, I've thought of another idea—

DR STOCKMANN: Good. Because I don't want to stay a moment longer than we need—

KATHERINE: Sssh! – Isn't that someone knocking?

PETRA: Yes – I expect it's Uncle Peter.

DR STOCKMANN: Aah! (*Calls.*) Come in!

KATHERINE: Now Thomas dear, please promise me you won't—

Enter PETER STOCKMANN *from hall.*

PETER: Oh, I see you've got a visitor. Then, perhaps, I'd better—

DR STOCKMANN: No, it's quite all right – come in.

PETER: I was rather hoping to have a word with you in private . . .

KATHERINE: Oh well, that's easily arranged. – We can go into the sitting-room . . .

CAPT HORSTER: I'll come back later.

DR STOCKMANN: No – why do that? – Go in there with them, Captain Horster, I want to hear more about that – er – idea of yours—

CAPT HORSTER: All right then, I'll wait.

CAPT HORSTER *follows Mrs Stockmann and Petra into sitting-room.* PETER *stays but glances uncomfortably at the broken windows.*

DR STOCKMANN: I should put your hat on again, if I were you. I expect you'll find it a bit draughty in here today. I shouldn't like you to catch cold . . .

PETER: Thanks, I will. (*Does so.*) As a matter of fact, I think I caught a bit of a cold last night – I kept on shivering—

DR STOCKMANN: Really? I found it quite warm – in fact, almost too hot for comfort towards the end . . .

PETER: I'm sorry I couldn't prevent them from carrying things to extremes like that last night.

DR STOCKMANN: Is that why you've come here this morning – simply to tell me that?

PETER (*bringing out a large envelope*): No, I've come to give you this – it's from the Baths Committee. . . .

DR STOCKMANN: My dismissal, I suppose?

PETER: Yes – dated from today. (*Puts it down on writing-table.*) We're very sorry to have to do this – but, quite frankly, we daren't do otherwise – on account of public opinion.

DR STOCKMANN (*smiling*): Daren't? I seem to have heard that word before . . .

PETER: I hope you realize the position – *your* position. – You can't rely on any sort of practice here, now, y'know.

DR STOCKMANN: Oh, damn the practice! – And, what makes you so sure?

PETER: Well, the Householders' Association has started a house-to-house campaign; it's sending round a circular to all its members, urging them not to consult you; and it's pretty certain that not a single head of a family will risk refusing his signature – he simply daren't!

DR STOCKMANN: Oh, I can well believe that. But what about it?

PETER: Well, if you'll follow my advice, I think you should leave the town for a bit—

DR STOCKMANN: Yes. As a matter of fact, that had already occurred to me . . .

PETER: Good. And then when you've had, say, six months or so, to think it over – and if you could bring yourself to write a few lines of apology and to admit you were mistaken—

DR STOCKMANN: I might perhaps be reappointed, you think?

PETER: Perhaps – it's certainly not impossible . . .

DR STOCKMANN: Yes – but what about public opinion? Surely you wouldn't dare – on account of public opinion!

PETER: Oh, public opinion's a very capricious thing, Thomas. And, to be perfectly candid with you, it's of considerable importance to us to get some sort of admission like that from you in writing . . .

DR STOCKMANN: Yes, I can quite see that. I suppose you've forgotten what I said to you the other day about tricks of that sort?

PETER: Ah, but your position was rather different then. You thought you had the whole town at your back—

DR STOCKMANN: Yes, and now I've got the whole town *on* my back! (*Flares up.*) But I wouldn't do it – not if I had all the devils in Hell on my back! Never! – Never, I tell you!

PETER: A man with a family ought to think twice about things; he's no right to behave as you're doing. He's no right to, Thomas!

DR STOCKMANN: No right! There's only one thing in the world a man has no right to do. – And d'you know what that is?

PETER: No.

DR STOCKMANN: No – I'm sure you don't! Well, I'll tell you. A free man has no right to play about in the dirt; he has

no right to behave so that he ought to spit in his own face
because of it!

PETER: All that would sound very plausible, if there were no
other reason for this obstinate attitude of yours; but, you
see, we all happen to know that there is—

DR STOCKMANN: And what, exactly, d'you mean by that?

PETER: You know quite well what I mean. But, as your
brother and as a man of the world, I advise you not to bank
too much on expectations . . .

DR STOCKMANN: Expectations? – What in heaven's name
are you talking about?

PETER: Do you seriously expect me to believe that you're
ignorant of the terms of your father-in-law's will?

DR STOCKMANN: I know that what little he has is to go to
some charity or other. But what's that got to do with me?

PETER: Well, to begin with 'the little he has' isn't so very
little. Old Morten Kiil is quite a wealthy man!

DR STOCKMANN: Well, I must say that's news to me!

PETER: Is that so? Then I suppose it's also news to you that
quite a considerable portion of it is to go to your children,
you and your wife having a life-interest in the capital? You
don't mean to tell me he's never mentioned it?

DR STOCKMANN: Never – I give you my word! In fact, he
spends most of the time grumbling about his income-tax. . . .
But are you sure of this, Peter?

PETER: I have it from a completely reliable source.

DR STOCKMANN: Then, thank heaven, Kate's provided for –
and the children too! I must tell her— (*Calls.*) Kate! –
Katherine!—

PETER (*restraining him*): No, don't. I shouldn't say anything
about it just yet, if I were you . . .

Enter MRS STOCKMANN *in sitting-room doorway.*

KATHERINE: Yes dear, what is it?

DR STOCKMANN: Oh nothing – nothing, my dear – never
mind.

KATHERINE: Oh... (*Exit, shutting door after her.*)

DR STOCKMANN (*pacing*): Provided for, eh! – all of 'em provided for – and for life! Well, it's certainly a relief. It's a wonderful thing to know that!

PETER: Yes, it would be if you were certain of it! But old Kiil can alter his will any time he likes!

DR STOCKMANN: I know – but he won't do that, my dear Peter. You've no idea how delighted 'The Badger' was when I fell out with you and your sagacious friends.

PETER (*starting and eyeing him searchingly*): Ah – now that throws a new light on quite a number of things...

DR STOCKMANN: What things?

PETER: Why, the whole thing, of course! It's perfectly obvious! It was nothing but a carefully laid plot you'd hatched between you! This violent and unwarranted attack of yours – in the name of truth! – against the leading man of the town—

DR STOCKMANN: Go on—

PETER: —was simply the price you paid that vindictive old man for making his will in your favour!

DR STOCKMANN (*practically dumbfounded*): Peter – you're just about the lowest specimen of social muckworm I've ever come across in all my born days!

PETER: Right! – This is the end of our friendship. And you can take your dismissal as final! Now we know where we are – at least we've got something we *can* use against you! (*Turns and exit by hall door.*)

DR STOCKMANN: You ought to be ashamed of yourself! (*Calls.*) Kate – scrub the floor after him! Get that girl – what's-her-name? – with the soot on her nose – to do it at once! Scrub it all over!

KATHERINE (*off-stage, from sitting-room*): Sssh, Thomas— Don't shout like that!

Enter PETRA *in sitting-room doorway.*

PETRA: Father, grandfather's here – and wants to speak to you alone . . .

DR STOCKMANN: Of course – ask him to come in. (*Crosses to door.*) Good morning, father-in-law – come in. . . . (*Enter* MORTEN KIIL. *Closes door behind him.*) Well, and what can I do for you? – Won't you sit down?

MORTEN KIIL: No, I won't sit down. (*Looks around.*) Well, it certainly looks very nice and homely here today, Thomas.

DR STOCKMANN: Yes, doesn't it?

MORTEN KIIL: Healthy too – plenty of fresh air. Plenty of that oxygen you were talking about last night. Your conscience must be in pretty good health this morning, I should think, Thomas.

DR STOCKMANN: It is.

MORTEN KIIL: That's what I thought. (*Taps his breast-pocket.*) D'you know what I've got here?

DR STOCKMANN: A good conscience too, I hope.

MORTEN KIIL: Bah! – No, something much better than that! (*Brings out a fat wallet, opens it and displays a wad of papers.*)

DR STOCKMANN (*eyeing him in astonishment*): Shares in the Baths?

MORTEN KIIL: They weren't hard to get today.

DR STOCKMANN: And you've been *buying* . . .?

MORTEN KIIL: As many as I had the money to pay for.

DR STOCKMANN: But, my dear father-in-law, why? – You know the Baths are in a bad way!

MORTEN KIIL: If you only pull yourself together, and behave like a reasonable human being, the Baths can be in a good way again in next to no time!

DR STOCKMANN: But, you saw for yourself I did all I possibly could! I tell you, the people in this town are raving mad! – And that's putting it mildly!

MORTEN KIIL: Now, you said last night that my tannery's the worst of the lot. If that's so then, I, my father and his father before him, have been polluting the town for over a century – like three destroying angels! You don't imagine for one moment that I'm going to have a thing like that said about us and take it lying down, do you?

DR STOCKMANN: Unfortunately, I don't see what else you can do.

MORTEN KIIL: You don't, eh? Well, we'll soon see about that! I think a lot of my good name and reputation, let me tell you! For too many years I've been known as 'The Badger'. – That's a kind of pig, I believe. Well, now I intend to put a stop to that, once and for all! I've been a clean man all my life and I mean to die one! I'll give 'em 'Badger'!

DR STOCKMANN: And how are you going to do it?

MORTEN KIIL: I'm not! – You're going to do it for me, Thomas.

DR STOCKMANN: I?

MORTEN KIIL: Yes, you – my son-in-law! D'you know what I bought these shares with? – No, of course you don't – but I'll tell you – with the money I was going to leave to Kate and the children, when I've gone. Oh, I managed to put by a little bit, y'know.

DR STOCKMANN (*flaring up*): And you've gone and done that with Kate's money!

MORTEN KIIL: That's right. Every penny of it's invested in the Baths now. And so now I want to see just how mad you are, Thomas! If you persist in this theory of yours that this muck and these microbes, or animals, or whatever they are, come mostly from my works, it'll be just like stripping the skin from Kate's body and Petra's and the boys' – and no decent father'ld ever do that unless he was stark, staring mad!

DR STOCKMANN (*pacing*): Yes, and that's just about what I am – I am mad...!

MORTEN KIIL: But not when it comes to your wife and children. You surely can't be such a raving lunatic as all that!

DR STOCKMANN (*stopping in front of him*): Why on earth

didn't you come and tell me you were going to buy up all that rubbish?

MORTEN KIIL: What's done can't be undone.

DR STOCKMANN (*pacing restlessly*): If only I weren't so certain about it. But I know, I'm absolutely convinced I'm right!

MORTEN KIIL (*weighing his wallet in his hand*): If you go on being mad like that, then these shares aren't worth the paper they're written on. . . . (*Puts wallet back in pocket.*)

DR STOCKMANN: But, hang it all! Surely science ought to be able to discover some sort of antidote – some sort of germicide, perhaps—

MORTEN KIIL: To kill these microbes and things, you mean?

DR STOCKMANN: Well, yes – or at least to render them harmless.

MORTEN KIIL: What about rat-poison?

DR STOCKMANN: Oh, don't be absurd! Anyhow, since everyone will have it that it's nothing but imagination on my part, let's leave it at that! Let 'em have their own way! After all, didn't the ignorant curs call me an enemy of the people – and try to tear the clothes off my back?

MORTEN KIIL: Yes, and not only that, they've smashed your windows for you too, y'know!

DR STOCKMANN: I haven't forgotten. And then there's my duty to my family. I must have a word with Kate about it, she knows more about these things than I do.

MORTEN KIIL: That's the idea – you take the advice of a sensible woman.

DR STOCKMANN (*approaching him*): But how could you do such a damn foolish thing, that's what I'ld like to know! – risking Kate's money and placing me in a devil of a dilemma like this! When I look at you, you might *be* the devil!

MORTEN KIIL: Well, I think I'd better go. But you must let me know without fail one way or the other by two o'clock.

And if it's no, then all the shares go to charity, and this afternoon at that . . . !

DR STOCKMANN: And then what'll Kate get?

MORTEN KIIL: Nothing – not a brass farthing! (*Hall door opens and enter* MESSRS HOVSTAD *and* ASLAKSEN *on threshold.*) Well, look what callers you've got now!

DR STOCKMANN (*staring at them*): What the—! Have you actually got the face to come here, both of you!

MR HOVSTAD: But, of course . . .

MR ASLAKSEN: You see, there's something we want to talk to you about . . .

MORTEN KIIL (*whispering*): Yes or no, without fail, before two o'clock.

MR ASLAKSEN (*glancing at Mr Hovstad*): Aah!
    Exit MORTEN KIIL *by hall door.*

DR STOCKMANN: Well? What d'you want? – And be brief!

MR HOVSTAD: I can quite understand your feeling angry with us over our attitude at the meeting last night, Doctor. . . .

DR STOCKMANN: Attitude, you call it? – A fine attitude! – You're nothing but a couple of cowardly old women, both of you! – and you ought to be ashamed of yourselves!

MR HOVSTAD: You can say what you like. The fact is, our hands were tied, and we couldn't do anything else.

DR STOCKMANN: You daren't, I suppose? Is that it?

MR HOVSTAD: Yes – if you want to put it like that.

MR ASLAKSEN: But why didn't you drop a hint to one of us beforehand – the merest hint to Mr Hovstad or to me—

DR STOCKMANN: Hint? What about?

MR ASLAKSEN: About what was behind it all.

DR STOCKMANN: I don't understand. – What on earth are you talking about?

MR ASLAKSEN (*nodding confidentially*): Oh yes, you do, Doctor Stockmann. . . .

MR HOVSTAD: It's no good trying to keep it a secret any longer.

DR STOCKMANN (*looking from one to the other*): What in the name of—!

MR ASLAKSEN: Isn't it a fact that your father-in-law's going round the town buying up all the shares in the Baths he can lay hands on?

DR STOCKMANN: Yes – he has been buying bath shares this morning, but—

MR ASLAKSEN: It would have been more discreet, y'know, to have got someone else to do it – someone not so closely related to you.

MR HOVSTAD: And you should really have kept your own name out of it. After all, it wasn't necessary for anyone to know that the attack on the Baths actually came from you. You should have taken me into your confidence, Doctor Stockmann.

DR STOCKMANN (*staring ahead, at first uncomprehendingly, then, amazedly*): Is this possible? – Can such things really happen? . . .

MR ASLAKSEN (*smiling*): It's obvious that they can. But really, Doctor, they should be done with a little finesse, y'know . . .

MR HOVSTAD: And it's always better to have a few others in it with you – to share the responsibility.

DR STOCKMANN (*calmly*): In a word, gentlemen – what, exactly, do you want?

MR ASLAKSEN: I think perhaps Mr Hovstad had better—

MR HOVSTAD: No, you – you tell him, Aslaksen—

MR ASLAKSEN: Well, the fact is: – now that we know what it's all about, we feel we might risk putting *The Herald* at your disposal. . . .

DR STOCKMANN: You dare to now, eh? But what about public opinion? Aren't you afraid of the storm that'll break over our heads?

MR HOVSTAD: We shall have to ride it out, that's all!

MR ASLAKSEN: And you, Doctor, must be ready to put, so to

speak, your helm hard over – and quickly! The moment we feel that your attack's achieved its maximum effect—

DR STOCKMANN: As soon as my father-in-law and I have bought all we can get in a falling market, you mean?

MR HOVSTAD: I presume that it's chiefly on scientific grounds that you wish to get control of the Baths?

DR STOCKMANN: Oh, naturally – it was only on scientific grounds that I could get the old 'Badger' to go in with me. We'll patch up the supply-pipes here and there, dig a few impressive-looking holes on the beach, and it won't cost the town a penny. Don't you think that ought to do the trick?

MR HOVSTAD: Yes, it certainly sounds all right – so long as you have *The Herald* behind you, of course. . . .

MR ASLAKSEN: The press is a power in a free community like ours, y'know, Doctor.

DR STOCKMANN: Yes, I'm sure it is. – And so, of course, is public opinion. I take it, we may safely leave the House-holders' Association in your hands, Mr Aslaksen – you'll look after them all right?

MR ASLAKSEN: Oh yes – and the Temperance Society. You needn't worry about that . . .

DR STOCKMANN: But gentlemen, there is one thing that occurs to me, and, really, I hardly like to mention it, but – er – well – what return d'you—?

MR HOVSTAD: Naturally, we should prefer to *give* you our support, Doctor. But unfortunately *The Herald* isn't doing quite as well as it should – the circulation's been falling lately. It would be a thousand pities if we had to shut down now – when there's so much work to be done in the political field here . . .

DR STOCKMANN: Of course – I quite understand. It would be a sad day for a friend of the people like you, I fully appreciate that. (*Flares up.*) But, you see, I happen to be an enemy of the people! (*Strides round room.*) Where's the devil's my stick? – Where did I put it?

MR HOVSTAD: Your what?

MR ASLAKSEN: My dear Doctor—

DR STOCKMANN (*stopping*): And suppose I don't give you anything? Suppose I refuse to give you a penny-piece of the money I make out of it? Because if there's one thing we rich folk hate, it's parting with our money, y'know!

MR HOVSTAD: This business of the shares can be represented in two ways, remember!

DR STOCKMANN: Yes, and you're just the man to do it! If I don't come to the rescue of *The Herald*, you'll put the worst possible construction on it – you'll never give me a moment's peace, you'll hunt me, hound me down – oh, I know – catch me and throttle me as a dog does a rabbit!

MR HOVSTAD: That applies to all animals, Doctor – it's one of the laws of nature – the law of self-preservation!

MR ASLAKSEN: And an animal has to take food where it finds it, y'know.

DR STOCKMANN: Then go and look for yours in the gutter! Because I'm now going to prove to you which is the strongest animal of us three! (*Finds umbrella and brandishes it.*) Now, let's just see—

MR HOVSTAD: Look here, Doctor, you're surely not going to—

MR ASLAKSEN: Be careful with that umbrella, Doctor, you might—

DR STOCKMANN: Out you go now, Hovstad – through the window – go on! – Jump for it!

MR HOVSTAD (*edging to hall door*): Have you gone mad?

DR STOCKMANN: And you too, Aslaksen – look lively! – Go on – jump! – through the window with you—

MR ASLAKSEN (*retreating round writing-table*): Moderation now, Doctor – moderation! I'm not a strong man, y'know – my legs, I— (*Calls.*) Help, help! Rescue! Help!

    Enter MRS STOCKMANN, PETRA *and* CAPT HORSTER *from sitting-room.*

KATHERINE: What ever's the matter, Thomas? – What on earth—?

DR STOCKMANN (*brandishing umbrella*): Jump, I say! – Go on – jump! – Into the gutter!

MR HOVSTAD: Attempted assault! – Unprovoked assault! – I call you to witness. Captain Horster! (*Slips out quickly into hall and exit.*)

MR ASLAKSEN (*helplessly, edging towards sitting-room door*): Oh, there must be a way out somewhere! (*Sneaks through sitting-room door and exit.*)

KATHERINE (*holding back Dr Stockmann*): Now Thomas, please – don't be silly . . .

DR STOCKMANN (*throwing aside umbrella*): Damn them! They've got away!

KATHERINE: But why? What was the matter? – What have they done?

DR STOCKMANN: I'll tell you later – I've other things to think about just now . . . (*Crosses to writing-table and scribbles on a visiting-card.*) Look, Kate – d'you see what I've written here?

KATHERINE (*looking*): Yes – three big noes. – What do they mean?

DR STOCKMANN: I'll tell you that later too. (*Hands cards to Petra.*) Here, Petra – tell sooty-nose to run round to 'The Badger's' with it, as quick as she can. Hurry now! (*Exit* PETRA *quickly by hall door.*) Well, if I haven't had visits today from every one of the devil's disciples! But now they're going to find out that a pen's mightier than an umbrella! I'll dip it in gall and venom, and then hurl the ink-pot straight at their heads!

KATHERINE: Yes, but I thought we were going away, Thomas?

Enter PETRA *by hall door.*

DR STOCKMANN: Well?

PETRA: She's taken it.

DR STOCKMANN: Good. Going away, did you say? No, I'm damned if we are! – We're staying here, Kate!

PETRA: Staying!

KATHERINE: Here, in this town?

DR STOCKMANN: Yes, here. This is the arena, and this is where I've got to fight! And what's more this is where I shall win! As soon as you've mended my trousers, I shall go out and start looking for a house – we must have a roof over our heads for the winter.

CAPT HORSTER: If that's all you want, you can have my house.

DR STOCKMANN: Can we? Really?

CAPT HORSTER: Yes – quite easily. There's plenty of room – and, anyhow, I'm hardly ever there . . .

KATHERINE: Well, that is good of you, Captain Horster.

PETRA: Oh, thank you!

DR STOCKMANN (*shaking hands with him*): Thanks, thanks, Horster! Well, that's one thing less to think about. Now I can get to work! – You've no idea how much there is to be done, Kate! Fortunately, I shall have plenty of time now. – I've been dismissed from the baths, y'know.

KATHERINE (*sighing*): Yes, I expected that.

DR STOCKMANN: And now they want to rob me of the practice as well! Well, they're welcome to it! The poor'll stick by me – those that can't pay! – And, hang it all, they're the ones that need me most! Oh, but they'll have to listen to me – I'll preach to them 'in season and out of season' – or whatever the phrase is!

KATHERINE: But Thomas dear, I should have thought you'ld have seen by now how much good preaching does.

DR STOCKMANN: Don't be silly, Kate! Am I to let myself be beaten by public opinion, the 'solid majority' and all the rest of the rubbish? No, thank you! What I want to do is clear, simple and straightforward. I just want to drum into their idiotic heads that their 'Liberals' are the wiliest enemies of freedom, that party programmes smother the truth – however vital it is, and that too great a consideration for expediency simply turns justice and morality upside-down until life becomes absolutely impossible. Hang it all! I ought to be able to convince them of that, don't you think, Captain Horster?

CAPT HORSTER: Perhaps – I should think so. I don't know very much about these things. . . .

DR STOCKMANN: You see, it's like this. – It's the party leaders that must be got rid of. Party leaders are like hungry wolves – they must devour a certain number of weaker victims every year in order to exist! Take Messrs Hovstad and Aslaksen! Look at the number they've finished off, or at least bitten and mauled so that they're useless except as householders and subscribers to *The Herald*! (*Sits on edge of table.*) Come here, Kate – look at that glorious sunshine – and take a good, deep breath of this marvellous spring air – this fresh air – isn't it wonderful?

KATHERINE: Yes, if only we could live on fresh air and sunshine, Thomas!

DR STOCKMANN: Well, you'll just have to pinch and scrape a bit – but we'll manage somehow. I'm not in the least worried about that. What bothers me is who's going to be broad-minded and courageous enough to carry on the good work when I'm gone . . .

PETRA: Oh, I shouldn't worry about that, Father – you've years and years ahead of you yet! . . . That sounds like the boys – Surely they aren't back from school already? . . .
    Enter EILIF *and* MORTEN *by sitting-room door.*

KATHERINE: Have you got a holiday today, then?

MORTEN: No – but we had a fight with some of the other boys in morning break—

EILIF: Oh, rot! – it was the other boys that started fighting with us!

MORTEN: All right, then. – And then Mr Rörlund told us we'd better stay at home for a few days . . .

DR STOCKMANN (*snapping his fingers and jumping up off the table*): That's it! – I've got it! By heaven, I've got it! You'll never set foot in that school again, either of you!

BOYS (*simultaneously*): Never? Aren't we going back to school?

KATHERINE: But Thomas—

DR STOCKMANN: No, never! – I'll teach you myself – that's to say, *I* shan't teach you anything!

MORTEN: Hooray!

DR STOCKMANN: —but at least you shall learn to be broad-minded and courageous men! And there's a job for *you*, Petra – you can help me!

PETRA: But of course I will, Father – I'ld love to!

DR STOCKMANN: And we'll start our school in the very room where they called me an enemy of the people. But two of you aren't enough – we must have at least a dozen to begin with—

KATHERINE: But you'll never get them, dear – not in this town . . .

DR STOCKMANN: Don't you believe it, Kate! (*To the boys.*) Don't you know any of the local street arabs? – Any of the real little devils? – Eh?

MORTEN: Yes, rather! – I know lots!

DR STOCKMANN: Good! Later on you shall go out and see what you can find . . . Experimenting with mongrels – just for once – might be quite interesting – *sometimes* they've got heads on their shoulders. . . .

MORTEN: But Father, what are we going to do when we've grown up into broad-minded and courageous men?

DR STOCKMANN: Drive all the wolves away, my lads!

KATHERINE: That is, if the wolves don't drive you away first, Thomas.

DR STOCKMANN: Don't be mad, Kate! Drive me away!

What now? Why, I'm the strongest man in town now!

KATHERINE: The strongest? – *now*?

DR STOCKMANN: Yes – in fact I'ld go so far as to say I'm perhaps the strongest man in the world!

MORTEN: I say, Father!

DR STOCKMANN (*quietly*): Ssh! – Now you mustn't tell anyone about it– not just yet, anyhow – but I've made a truly great discovery ...!

KATHERINE: Oh no – not another one, dear?

DR STOCKMANN: Yes – another one, Kate. (*Gathers them round him; confidentially.*) And this is it – the strongest man in the world is he who stands alone!

KATHERINE (*smiling and shaking her head*): Oh, Thomas, Thomas—

PETRA (*grasping his hands warmly*): Father!

CURTAIN